SO-BBC-192

Essential
Australia

AAA Publishing 1000 AAA Drive, Heathrow, Florida 32746

Australia: Regions and Best places to see

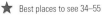 Best places to see 34–55

Original text by Anne Matthews
Updated by Marie Hall

American editor: G.K. Sharman

Edited, designed and produced by AA Publishing
© Automobile Association Developments Limited 2007
Maps © Automobile Association Developments Limited 2007

This edition printed 2007, reprinted Oct 2007

ISBN-13: 978-1-59508-173-5
ISBN-10: 1-59508-173-9

Published in the United States by AAA Publishing,
1000 AAA Drive, Heathrow, Florida 32746
Published in the United Kingdom by AA Publishing

Color separation: MRM Graphics Ltd
Printed and bound in Italy by Printer Trento S.r.l.

A03164
Maps in this title produced from map data © New Holland Publishing (South Africa)
(Pty) Ltd. 2005
Transport map © Communicarta Ltd, UK

About this book

This book is divided into five sections.

The essence of Australia pages 6–19
Introduction; Features; Food and Drink;
Short Break including the 10 Essentials

Planning pages 20–33
Before You Go; Getting There; Getting
Around; Being There

Best places to see pages 34–55
The unmissable highlights of any visit
to Australia

Best things to do pages 56–77
Good places to have lunch; top
activities; great views; places to take
the children; exceptional lesser-known
destinations and more

Exploring pages 78–187
The best places to visit in Australia,
organized by area

Maps
All map references are to the maps on
the covers. For example, Melbourne has
the reference ✚ 21J – indicating the
grid square in which it is to be found.

Prices
An indication of the cost of restaurants
and cafés at attractions is given by
$** signs: **$$$ denotes higher prices,
$$ denotes average prices,
$ denotes lower prices.

Hotel prices
Per room per night: **$** budget (under
AU$120); **$$** moderate (AU$120–$240);
$$$ expensive to luxury (over AU$240).

Restaurant prices
Price for a three-course meal per person
without drinks: **$** budget (under AU$30);
$$ moderate (AU$30–$50);
$$$ expensive (over AU$50).

Contents

The essence of...

Visitors come to Australia for many reasons, but the continent's greatest appeal is undoubtedly its 'Great Outdoors'. The climate is generally warm and balmy, and the magnificent scenery includes rugged sandstone peaks and escarpments, rainforests, harsh Outback deserts, white-sand beaches and clear tropical waters. The unique plants, birds and animals add an exotic touch to an already dramatic landscape.

There are also many historical and cultural experiences to be savoured in Australia. The locals are friendly, warm and welcoming, and this relaxed atmosphere is complemented by fabulous food and wine. A visit 'Down Under' may well surprise you with its variety of experiences.

THE ESSENCE OF AUSTRALIA

features

From its unpromising convict beginnings, Australia has developed into a wealthy and politically stable nation of over 20 million people. Since the early days of dependence on Britain, the national self-esteem has grown decade by decade over the past 200 or so years, and people from all over the world have settled here, making Australia today a vibrant, diverse and confident nation.

Australia – variously known as 'Down Under', 'Oz', and the 'best address on earth' – is vast: approximately 24 times the size of the British Isles and as big as continental USA (without Alaska). The terrain and climate obviously vary considerably, but overall the weather is warm and sunny, and the scenery varies from interesting to magnificent.

This benign climate has undoubtedly affected the Australian character, best described as egalitarian and relaxed. Aussies are friendly and laid-back, and visitors from everywhere are welcomed enthusiastically. This is a multicultural nation where, despite some intolerance towards Indigenous people in particular, people of European, Asian, Arabic, Pacific Island and other origins live together in relative harmony.

Visitors should remember that Australia is enormous – it is over 4,000km (2,485 miles) from Sydney to Perth – so unless you have months to spare, select your destinations carefully.

NATURAL FEATURES

- Australia is the world's smallest and flattest continent and, after Antarctica, the driest.
- Australia's mainland coastline is a huge 36,700km (22,800 miles).
- Australia's highest point is Mount Kosciuszko in southern New South Wales – a mere 2,228m (7,310ft) high. The lowest point is 16m (52ft) below sea level at Lake Eyre in Outback South Australia.
- The Great Barrier Reef is the world's largest living, growing structure – it is composed primarily of coral polyps and algae and stretches for over 2,000km (1,240 miles) along the Queensland coast.
- The continent has over 15,000 flowering plant species, including over 700 varieties of eucalyptus.

MAKE-UP AND PEOPLE

- There are six states: New South Wales, Queensland, Victoria, Tasmania, South Australia and Western Australia; two territories: the Australian Capital Territory and the Northern Territory; and external territories, including Norfolk Island and Christmas Island.
- Although of a similar size to the United States (population over 250 million), and 24 times the size of Britain, Australia is home to only 20 million people. Just over 4 million live in Sydney.
- In 2001 the number of overseas-born Australians was 4.5 million (23 per cent of the population), and 26 per cent of those born here had at least one overseas-born parent.

ROAD AND RAIL

- Australia has more than 810,000km (503,335 miles) of roads, but only 35 per cent are sealed.
- The world's longest straight stretch of railway is in Outback Western Australia – it is 478.4km (297 miles) long.

food & drink

It seems almost inconceivable that in the early 1980s Australian food was bland and very much of the traditional English 'meat and two veg' school of cooking: sweet and sour pork or a prawn cocktail were considered the height of culinary sophistication. All this has changed dramatically, largely due to Asian, Middle Eastern and European immigrants introducing their ingredients and styles of cooking.

A WORLD OF FOOD

Australian cuisine is now taking the world by storm – the famous chef Robert Carrier predicted on a visit in 1996 that Australian food was the most exciting available, and that it was about to take over the world. Much of this acclaim is due to the

development and refinement of 'Modern Australian' cuisine – a form of cooking that has evolved from the use of excellent fresh produce, the fusion of styles and ingredients (anything from Thai to French in one dish), and stylish presentation.

An important component of Australia's inventive cuisine is the superb quality and variety of local produce, from tropical fruits like mangoes to Tasmania's wonderful cheeses and the freshest herbs. The quality of meat is very high, and the variety of seafood will astonish many northern hemisphere visitors: enormous prawns, oysters, crabs, lobsters and delicious tropical fish such as barramundi.

Australia also offers cuisines from all over the world, with Thai, Japanese and other Asian restaurants being particularly popular. You will find everything from Italian and Greek to Lebanese

and African cuisines, and one of the greatest joys in this fine climate is eating al fresco, often with a marvellous sea view.

WINE, BEER AND SPIRITS

Wine has been produced in Australia since the late 1830s, and the country's reds and whites are now deservedly world famous. All of the states have some involvement in the industry, but South Australia's Barossa Valley and Coonawarra region, the Hunter Valley of New South Wales, and the Margaret River area of Western Australia are some of the most famous.

Red varieties include Cabernet Sauvignon, Shiraz, Pinot Noir and Merlot, while Chardonnay,

Chablis, Sauvignon Blanc and Verdelho are popular whites. There are many hundreds of different labels to choose from, and the best way to discover what you like is to try as many as possible! Ultimately, it all comes down to taste, but it's hard to go wrong with labels like Wolf Blass, Rosemount Estate, Penfolds, Houghtons and Henschke.

Australian beers are now known throughout the world, and there is a huge range to choose from. In addition to Fosters, Tooheys, VB (Victoria Bitter), Reschs, Cascade, Carlton, Swan and XXXX (Fourex) there are popular regional brands, and aficionados will enjoy specialist beers like Hahn, Coopers, Redback and the curiously named Dogbolter. Australia is not renowned for its spirits, although reasonably good brandy is produced in South Australia. Sampling Bundaberg rum – universally known as 'Bundy' and a delicious by-product of the sugar industry in Queensland – is a must. This fine spirit comes as both underproof (37 per cent) and overproof (a lethal 57.7 per cent), and is usually mixed with cola.

short break

If you only have a short time to visit Australia and would like to take home some unforgettable memories, you can do something local and capture the real flavour of the country. The following suggestions will give you a wide range of sights and experiences that won't take very long, won't cost very much and will make your visit very special. If you only have time to choose one of these, you will have found the true heart of Australia.

● **Take a cruise on Sydney Harbour** (➤ 50–51) and enjoy the beautiful scenery at the heart of the city.

● **Spend a day at the beach** to experience the sun, surf and sheer hedonism of Bondi (➤ 82) or any other of Australia's magnificent beaches. You could even have a go at surfing.

● **See a performance at the Sydney Opera House,** where you can enjoy the acclaimed Australian Ballet, Opera Australia or Sydney Symphony Orchestra inside the nation's most distinctive building (➤ 50–51).

● **Experience the Great Barrier Reef** – snorkel or dive among the colourful coral and luminous fish of the eighth wonder of the world (➤ 42–43).

● **Dine al fresco** to sample Modern Australian cuisine, especially some of the wonderful seafood, at an outdoor table with a view across the coast.

● **Visit Uluru** – at the very heart of the continent, the world's largest monolith exudes an awesome sense of mystery and timelessness (➤ 54–55).

● **Learn about Australia's history** – discover something of pre-European Aboriginal life at the Australian Museum (➤ 83), and head to Port Arthur (➤ 142) for an insight into the harsh convict days.

● **Go bushwalking** – a hike in the bush (countryside) is a must. Explore the escarpments and eucalypt forests of the Blue Mountains (➤ 36–37).

● **Visit a wildlife park** for a close encounter with kangaroos, emus, wombats, koalas and other unique Australian fauna (➤ 70–71, 87).

● **Sample local wines and beers** – spend an evening in an Aussie pub, meet the locals, and enjoy world-class wines and fine beers.

Planning

Before You Go

WHEN TO GO

JAN	FEB	MAR	APR	MAY	JUN	JUL	AUG	SEP	OCT	NOV	DEC
26°C	26°C	25°C	22°C	19°C	17°C	16°C	18°C	20°C	22°C	24°C	25°C
79°F	79°F	77°F	72°F	66°F	63°F	61°F	65°F	68°F	72°F	75°F	77°F

High season   Low season

The temperatures listed above are the **average daily maximum** for each month in Sydney. Australia has a range of climates because of its size, geographical location and lack of high mountain ranges.

During the summer months (December to February) the southern states are the best places to visit, while Western Australia, the Northern Territory and

Queensland are hot and humid. November to April is the wet season in northern Queensland and parts of Western Australia and the Northern Territory, bringing tropical cyclones. Most of the rainfall in the Great Barrier Reef occurs in January and February.

Winter (June to August) is the best time to visit the north, west and Red Centre.

WHAT YOU NEED

● Required
○ Suggested
▲ Not required

Some countries require a passport to remain valid for a minimum period (usually at least six months) beyond the date of entry contact their consulate or embassy or your travel agent for details.

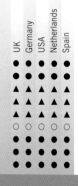

	UK	Germany	USA	Netherlands	Spain
Passport (or National Identity Card where applicable)	●	●	●	●	●
Visa (regulations can change – check before you travel)	●	●	●	●	●
Onward or Return Ticket	▲	▲	▲	▲	▲
Health Inoculations (tetanus and polio)	▲	▲	▲	▲	▲
Health Documentation (► 23, Health Advice)	▲	▲	▲	▲	▲
Travel Insurance	○	○	○	○	○
Driving Licence (national) and International Driving Permit	●	●	●	●	●
Car Insurance Certificate	●	●	●	●	●
Car Registration Document	●	●	●	●	●

ADVANCE PLANNING
WEBSITES

www.australia.com
www.planbooktravel.com

TOURIST OFFICES AT HOME

In the UK
Australian Tourist Commission
✉ Gemini House
10–18 Putney Hill
London SW15 6AA
☎ 020 8780 2229

In the USA
Australian Tourist Commission
✉ 2049 Century Park East
Suite 1920
Los Angeles CA 90067
☎ 310/229 4870

HEALTH ADVICE
Insurance
British and certain other nationals
are eligible for free basic care at
public hospitals but it is strongly
recommended that all travellers
take out a comprehensive medical
insurance policy.

Dental services
Dentists are plentiful and the
standard of treatment is high –
as are the bills. In an emergency
go to the casualty wing
(emergency room) of a local
hospital, or locate a dentist from
the local telephone book. Medical
insurance is essential.

TIME DIFFERENCES

GMT	Sydney	Germany	USA (NY)	Netherlands	Spain
12 noon	10PM	1PM	7AM	1PM	1PM

Australia has three time zones.
The eastern states and ACT follow
Eastern Standard Time, which is
10 hours ahead of GMT (GMT+10).
South Australia and the Northern
Territory follow Central Standard
Time (GMT+9:30) and Western

Australia follows Western Standard
Time (GMT+8).
   Daylight Saving Time varies from
state to state and is not observed in
Western Australia, Queensland and
the Northern Territory.

WHAT'S ON WHEN

As a nation, Australia spends a considerable amount of time in holiday and party mode. There are nine annual national public holidays, and each state holds at least one major festival each year. These range from the highbrow Adelaide, Melbourne and Sydney arts festivals to sporting carnivals and the bizarre Henley-on-Todd Regatta at waterless Alice Springs.

January

Mid- to late Jan: *Australian Open* (tennis), Melbourne.
January 26: *Australia Day* holiday.
All month: *Sydney Festival* (performing arts).

February

Chinese New Year, around Australia.
End Feb: *Gay and Lesbian Mardi Gras*, Sydney.
Tropfest (short film festival), various capital cities.
Feb/Mar: *Adelaide Festival of Arts* and *Adelaide Fringe Festival* (even-numbered years only).
Perth International Arts Festival.

March

Early Mar: *Australian Formula One Grand Prix*, Melbourne.
Early to mid-Mar: *Canberra National Multicultural Festival*.

WOMADelaide (world music festival), Adelaide.
Late Mar or early Apr: *Barossa Vintage Festival* (odd-numbered years only), Barossa Valley.
Royal Easter Show, Sydney.

April

April 25: *Anzac Day* holiday.
Variable: *Melbourne International Comedy Festival*.
East Coast Roots and Blues Festival, Byron Bay.

May

Early May: *Bangtail Muster*, Alice Springs.

June

Wintersun Carnival, Gold Coast.
Variable: *Out of the Box Festival* for 3–8 year olds (even-numbered years), Brisbane.

July

Mid-Jul: *Camel Cup Carnival* (camel races), Alice Springs.
Darwin Cup Carnival (horse races).

NATIONAL HOLIDAYS

JAN	FEB	MAR	APR	MAY	JUN	JUL	AUG	SEP	OCT	NOV	DEC
2		(2)	1(3)		1						2

1 January	New Year's Day
26 January	Australia Day
March/April	Good Friday
March/April	Easter Monday
25 April	Anzac Day
Second Mon in June	Queen's Birthday
(WA: last Mon in Sep)	
25 December	Christmas Day
26 December	Boxing Day

In addition, individual states have public holidays throughout the year for agricultural shows, eg Brisbane Royal Show, Royal Canberra Show, Alice Springs and Hobart shows; regattas and race days, eg Melbourne Cup Day, Adelaide Cup Day and Hobart Regatta Day.

Late July: *Royal Darwin Show.*
Brisbane Festival (performing arts, even-numbered years).

August
Mid-Aug: *City to Surf* (fun run), Sydney.
Aug to Sep: *Festival of Darwin.*
Late Aug: *Alice Springs Rodeo.*

September
Late Sep: *AFL Grand Final* (Australian Rules football), Melbourne.
Mid-Sep to mid-Oct: *Floriade Spring Festival,* Canberra.
Henley-on-Todd Regatta, Alice Springs.
Festival Cairns (performing arts).

October
Mid-Oct: *Gold Coast Indy Carnival* (motor race).
Manly International Jazz Festival, Sydney.
Melbourne International Arts Festival.

November
First Tue: *Melbourne Cup* (horse race).
Late Nov: *Fremantle Festival.*

December
Late Dec: *Hobart Summer Festival.*

Getting There

BY AIR

All major airlines operate services to Australia. Qantas, the Australian national airline, flies from London to Australia's international airports. Flights from Europe take between 20 and 30 hours; flights from North America take about 15 hours. Many other international carriers such as British Airways, Singapore Air, Malaysia Airlines and Cathay Pacific fly to state capitals, with Melbourne and Sydney being the busiest. All have good facilities and links to their major cities.

NEW SOUTH WALES
Sydney Airport

The Sydney Airport (**www**.sydneyairport.com.au) is located 10km (6 miles) from the city centre and can be reached by taxi, bus or train.

The Sydney Airporter bus runs every 15 minutes and operates a door-to-door service from the airport to a variety of accommodation in the city, around Darling Harbour and Kings Cross.

A train service – the Airport Link (**www**.airportlink.com.au) – runs a fast service straight into Central Station every 10–15 minutes during peak times.

Melbourne Airport

Melbourne Airport (**www**.melair.com.au) is slightly further out of the city, being 25km (15 miles) away, and can be reached by taxi or shuttlebus.

Taxis are expensive but the most convenient form of transfer, whereas the Skybus Super Shuttle (**www**.skybus.com.au) is less expensive and operates a 24-hour service between Melbourne airport and Southern Cross Station downtown. Buses depart from the airport every 15 minutes between 6am and 9pm and once hourly between 1am and 5am.

There is also a free minibus shuttle service between Southern Cross Station and hotels in the Central Business District (CBD).

QUEENSLAND
Brisbane

Situated 13km (8 miles) from the city, Brisbane Airport (**www**.bne.com.au) can be reached by taxi, train and bus.

Taxis are direct but expensive and can be found outside all terminals.

Airtrain (**www**.airtrain.com.au) is a fast and effective service that runs every 15 minutes from outside the terminals at the domestic and international airports. Trains stop at Bowen Hills, Brunswick Street, Central, Roma Street, South Brisbane and Southbank and run half-hourly to the Gold Coast.

The cheapest transfer option is to take the Skytrans shuttle bus which runs to the city every 30 minutes during the hours 5.45am to 11.15pm.

The Airporter bus is a transfer service that runs every hour to the Gold Coast but is very expensive.

Cairns
Also in Queensland, Cairns Airport (www.cairnsairport.com.au) is 7km (5 miles) outside the town and can easily be reached by taxi. The airport shuttle bus service, Cairns Airporter Shuttle bus, operates inexpensive transfers between the airport and most hotels.

NORTHERN TERRITORY
Darwin
Some 12km (7 miles) from the city, Darwin Airport is easily reached by taxi (expensive) or the Darwin Airport Shuttle Service (inexpensive) which transfers from the airport to hotel accommodation.

SOUTH AUSTRALIA
Adelaide
Just 7km (4 miles) from the city, Adelaide Airport (www.aal.com.au) has good links to the city by taxi or by Skylink, a shuttle service running every half hour from 6am to 9.30pm Monday to Friday and hourly on the weekends.

WESTERN AUSTRALIA
Perth
Perth Airport (www.perthairport.net.au) is situated 20km (12 miles) from the city and can be reached by taxi (expensive) or the Perth Airport Shuttle bus (reasonable) which runs to Perth city as well as Fremantle, stopping at most central accommodation areas.

BY SEA
Many world cruises dock at major port cities in Australia as part of their itinerary. An informative website on sea travel is www.cruisecritic.com

Getting Around

PUBLIC TRANSPORT

Internal flights Australia has a wide network of domestic and regional air services. Qantas (**www**.qantas.com.au), Jetstar (**www**.jetstar.com.au) and Virgin Blue (**www**.virginblue.com. au) are the main domestic airlines, and often offer discount deals on accommodation and car rental as well as flights.

Trains Most capital cities have frequent services between business districts and the suburbs. Long-distance trains offer sleeping berths and reclining seats, and most interstate trains have dining or buffet cars. If you are booking ahead from outside Australia, enquries and reservations are handled by Rail Australia (**www**.railaustralia.com.au).

Bus travel Excellent long-distance express bus services run daily between major cities, serviced by McCafferty's Greyhound (☎ 132 030 or 131 499). Coaches are non-smoking, have air-conditioning and bathrooms. Tasmania is serviced by Tasmanian Redline Coaches (☎ 1300 360 000) and Tassie Link (☎ 03 6257 0293).

Ferries The only regular interstate ferry services are the overnight Spirit of Tasmania passenger/vehicle ferries between Melbourne and Devonport in Tasmania (daily service; twice daily during summer) and Sydney and Devonport (twice weekly in winter, three times weekly at other times). For more information, contact ☎ 1800 634 906; **www**.spiritoftasmania.com.au

Urban transport Most state capital cities have good train services and/or frequent bus services that operate between the city centre and the suburbs. Perth, Brisbane and Sydney also have regular local ferry services. Trams or light railways run in Melbourne, Adelaide and Sydney.
For transport information in Sydney: ☎ 131500; **www**.131500.com.au Melbourne: ☎ 131 638; **www**.metlinkmelbourne.com.au Perth: ☎ 13 62 13;

www.transperth.wa.gov.au
Brisbane: ☎ 13 12 30;
www.translink.com.au
Adelaide: ☎ (08) 0218 2362;
www.transadelaide.com.au

Taxis Except in some country towns, all taxis in Australia display the fare on a meter. Taxis can be booked or stopped on the street.

DRIVING
Drive on the left.

Car rental Rental cars are available at major air and rail terminals and from cities throughout Australia. It is advisable to book ahead, especially during December and January. Most rental companies offer advice and provide relevant guides and maps.

If your rental car breaks down you should contact the rental company, which will arrange to send road service to your location and repair the vehicle. Alternatively, most service stations will be able to assist or, at least, direct you to the nearest repair centre.

Speed limit on motorways:
100–110kph (62–68mph)
Speed limit on urban roads:
40–60kph (52–37mph)

Obey the speed limits. There are speed cameras throughout the country and hefty speeding fines.

It is compulsory to wear seat belts at all times.

Random breath-testing. Never drive under the influence of alcohol.

Filling stations are plentiful, except in some Outback areas, but business hours may vary. Most service stations accept international credit cards.

CONCESSIONS
Students/Youths Young visitors should join the International Youth Hostels Federation before leaving their own country. Australia has a widespread network of youth and backpacker hostels. International Student or Youth Identity Cards may entitle the holder to discounts.
Senior citizens Many attractions offer a discount for senior citizens; the age limit varies from 60–65. However, few discounts on travel are available to overseas senior citizens, as an Australian pension card is usually required to qualify.

Being There

TOURIST OFFICES

● Canberra Visitor Centre (ACT) ✉ 330 Northbourne Avenue, Dickson 2602 ☎ (02) 6205 0044 **www.**canberratourism.com.au

● Sydney Visitor Centre (NSW) ✉ Corner of Argyle and Playfair streets, The Rocks ☎ (02) 9240 8788; **www.**visitnsw.com.au

● Queensland Travel Centre ✉ 30 Makerston Street, Brisbane 4000 ☎ (07) 3535 4557; **www.**queenslandtravel.com

● Western Australia Visitor Centre ✉ Corner of Forrest Place and Wellington Street, Perth 6000 ☎ (08) 9483 1111; **www.**visitwa.com.au

● Tourism NT ✉ Tourism House, 43 Mitchell Street, Darwin 0800 ☎ (08) 8999 3900; **www.**tourismnt.com

● South Australia Visitor and Travel Centre ✉ 18 King William Street, Adelaide 3000 ☎ (08) 8303 2220; **www.**southaustralia.com

● Melbourne Visitor Information Centre ✉ Federation Square, Melbourne 3000 ☎ (03) 9658 9658; **www.**visitvictoria.com.au

● Tasmanian Travel and Information Centre ✉ 20 Davey Street, Hobart 7000 ☎ (03) 6230 8233 **www.**discovertasmania.com

EMBASSIES AND CONSULATES

UK ☎ (02) 6270 6666; Canberra
Germany ☎ (02) 6270 1911; Canberra
USA ☎ (02) 6214 5600; Canberra
Netherlands ☎ (02) 6273 3111; Canberra
Spain ☎ (02) 6273 3555; Canberra

TELEPHONES

Long-distance calls within Australia (STD) and International Direct Dialling (IDD) can be made on public payphones. Public payphones accept coins and various phonecards, which are available from retail outlets in denominations of AU$5, AU$10 and AU$20. The International Direct service gives access to over 50 countries for collect or credit card calls. Phones that accept credit cards can be found at airports, central city locations and hotels. A Telstra PhoneAway prepaid card

OPENING HOURS

- Shops
- Offices
- Banks
- Post Offices
- Mseums/Monuments
- Pharmacies

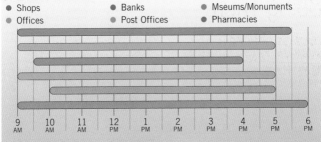

Shops: Hours vary from state to state. Many supermarkets and department stores stay open until 9pm on Thu and/or Fri. Some supermarkets in larger cities are open daily until midnight.

Banks: Open Mon–Fri 9–5. Some open Saturday morning.
Museums: Hours may vary.
Pharmacies: Some are open longer hours, including 24-hour services in larger cities.

enables you to use virtually any phone in Australia with all call costs charged to the card.

EMERGENCY TELEPHONE NUMBERS
Police: 000
Fire: 000
Ambulance: 000

INTERNATIONAL DIALLING CODES
To call from Australia to:
UK: 0011 44
Germany: 0011 49
USA/Canada: 0011 1
Netherlands: 0011 31
Spain: 0011 34

POSTAL SERVICES
Post offices Australia Post (**www.**auspost.com.au) offices can be found throughout the country; often combined with a general store in smaller places. Postal and poste restante services are available. Mail boxes are red with a white 'P'.

ELECTRICITY
The power supply is: 220/240 volts, 50 cycles AC.

Sockets accept three-flat-pin plugs so you may need an adaptor. If your appliances are 110v check if there is a 110/240v switch; if not you will need a voltage converter.

Universal outlets for 240v or 110v shavers are usually found in leading hotels.

CURRENCY AND FOREIGN EXCHANGE

The monetary unit of Australia is the Australian dollar (AU$) and the cent (100¢ = AU$1).

Coins come in 5¢, 10¢, 20¢, 50¢ and $1 and $2 denominations, and there are $5, $10, $20, $50 and $100 notes.

Major credit cards are accepted in all large cities and most airports and banks have facilities for changing foreign currency and traveller's cheques.

HEALTH AND SAFETY

Sun advice The sun in Australia is extremely strong, especially in summer. Wear a hat and sunglasses, and avoid sunbathing in the middle of the day. Use a high-SPF sunscreen.

Drugs Prescription and non-prescription drugs are available from pharmacies. Visitors may import up to three months' supply of prescribed medication: bring a doctor's certificate.

Safe water It is safe to drink tap water throughout Australia. Bottled mineral water is widely available.

Personal safety The usual safety precautions should be taken. Walking in the bush and swimming have their hazards.
● Hitchhiking is not recommended and is strongly discouraged by the Australian government.
● Women should avoid walking alone at night.
● If bushwalking or camping, leave an itinerary with friends. Wear boots, socks and trousers.

TIPS/GRATUITIES

Yes ✓ No ✕

Restaurants (if service not included)	✓	10%
Cafés/bars	✕	
Taxis	✕	
Porters	✓	$1–$2/bag
Chambermaids	✕	
Cloakroom attendants	✕	
Hairdressers	✕	
Theatre/cinema usherettes	✕	
Toilets	✕	

- Take care and heed warning signs when swimming, whether in the sea or fresh water (crocodiles!)
- Avoid swimming at beaches in the northern parts of Australia during the wet season (Nov–Apr), due to deadly box jellyfish.
- Surf only on patrolled beaches and stay between the flags.

PHOTOGRAPHY

What to photograph: The wilderness, Barrier Reef, mountains, natural scenery and modern architecture.

What not to photograph: Many Aboriginal people do not wish to be photographed. Always ask permission before taking photographs of Indigenous Australians or scared sites.

When to photograph: In the Outback the light can be intense; best to photograph early in the morning or late afternoon. Allow for reflected light at coastal locations.

MEDIA

What's on The entertainment scene in capital cities is covered by the major newspapers. The *Sydney Morning Herald* Metro section (in Friday's edition) is a comprehensive look at entertainment in Sydney during the next week. You can also visit **www.**citysearch.com.au for nationwide entertainment listings.

CLOTHING SIZES

Australia	UK	Europe	USA	
36	36	46	36	
38	38	48	38	
40	40	50	40	
42	42	52	42	
44	44	54	44	
46	46	56	46	**Suits**
7	7	41	8	
7.5	7.5	42	8.5	
8.5	8.5	43	9.5	
9.5	9.5	44	10.5	
10.5	10.5	45	11.5	
11	11	46	12	**Shoes**
14.5	14.5	37	14.5	
15	15	38	15	
15.5	15.5	39/40	15.5	
16	16	41	16	
16.5	16.5	42	16.5	
17	17	43	17	**Shirts**
8	8	34	6	
10	10	36	8	
12	12	38	10	
14	14	40	12	
16	16	42	14	
18	18	44	16	**Dresses**
6.5	4.5	38	6	
7	5	38	6.5	
7.5	5.5	39	7	
8	6	39	7.5	
8.5	6.5	40	8	
9	7	41	8.5	**Shoes**

Best places to see

1 Blue Mountains, New South Wales

www.bluemts.com.au

For a complete change to Sydney's waterfront glamour, visit these nearby mountains to experience the great natural beauty of their geological wonders.

This is one of Australia's most popular holiday destinations. Visitors come to the Blue Mountains to experience their wild grandeur, mist-filled valleys, rich Aboriginal and European heritage, and to escape the summer heat. The cold winters allow visitors to enjoy the charm of open fires. Just two hours by road or train from Sydney, the mountains get their name from their blue haze.

There is so much to do and see here, from just taking in the panoramic views from the many escarpment lookouts to walking in the temperate rainforests which line the ravines and valleys. Waterfalls cascade off the cliffs into valleys far below, where they join streams that

disappear into dense vegetation. The golden brown of ancient, weathered rock faces, formed by the action of the elements over millions of years, contrasts with the distinctive blue-green of the mountain vegetation.

Because of the great range and diversity of land forms and plant communities, and its habitats sheltering rare or endangered fauna, the Greater Blue Mountains region became a World Heritage Site in 2000. In addition to its natural sights and adventure sports, there are myriad galleries, antiques shops, gardens, museums and fine eating establishments to enjoy. The Katoomba Scenic Railway and the Sceniscender provide unique perspectives of their surroundings while just over the range are the famous Jenolan Caves with their amazing limestone formations.

🚹 23K 🚆 From Sydney; stops at various mountain towns. Driving is another option
❓ A wide range of accommodation from B&Bs to five star. Many tour companies operate day tours from Sydney
ℹ️ Information centres ✉ Great Western Highway, Glenbrook; ✉ Echo Point, Katoomba ☎ 1300 653 408 or 1800 641 227
🕐 Glenbrook: Mon–Fri 9–5, Sat–Sun 8.30–4.30. Closed 25 Dec

2 Cairns and District, North Queensland

www.tropicalaustralia.com.au

Cairns is the perfect base for a superb nature-based holiday allowing trips to the World Heritage-listed reefs and rainforests as well as the dry Outback.

With its international airport, well-developed tourism infrastructure and proximity to natural attractions such as the Great Barrier Reef, tropical rainforests and Atherton Tableland, Cairns is the 'tourist capital' of North Queensland. Here are dozens of hotels, restaurants and shops, and many options for cruises – as well as diving, fishing or

snorkelling trips – to the reef. Excellent beaches stretch to the north and south, and adventure activities like whitewater rafting and bungee jumping are popular. Around town you can visit the Cairns Museum and the Pier Marketplace, or just wander the streets and waterfront to soak up the city's relaxed, tropical atmosphere. North of the city is the pretty coastal town of Port Douglas, while further afield are Mossman and the Daintree rainforests.

Inland from Cairns, the cool upland region of the Atherton Tableland, with its fertile farming land, volcanic lakes, waterfalls and rainforest, presents a striking contrast to the hot, humid coast. Kuranda (27km/17 miles away) offers colourful markets, a fauna sanctuary and rainforest interpretation centre. You can reach Kuranda by road, on the spectacular Skyrail Rainforest Cableway, or by travelling on the famous Kuranda Scenic Railway, which winds its way up the Great Dividing Range.

For a complete change, take a trip inland to the Gulf Savannah country and sample the hospitality of the Outback locals. Discover the grasslands, wetlands, escarpments and the Undara Lava Tubes.

🚑 10D 💲 Inexpensive–expensive ✖ Cairns
❓ Huge variety of accommodation from backpacker to five star. Car rental is relatively expensive but there are many bus services and tours to all popular destinations
ℹ Tourism Tropical North Queensland ✉ 51 The Esplanade, Cairns ☎ (07) 4051 3588 🕐 Daily; Port Douglas Tourist Information Centre ✉ 23 Macrossan Street, Port Douglas ☎ (07) 4099 5599 🕐 Daily; Kuranda Visitor Information Centre ☎ (07) 4093 311 🕐 Daily

3 Gold Coast, Queensland

www.goldcoasttourism.com.au

Although not to everyone's liking, the brash and sometimes crass Gold Coast reveals a very different side of Australia from its natural wonders.

It would be difficult not to have a good time on this lively, highly developed 70km (43-mile) strip of coastline to the south of Brisbane. Stretching down to Coolangatta on the New South Wales border, the Gold Coast offers consistently warm temperatures and an average of 300 days of sunshine each year. The sandy beaches are lapped by clear blue waters that are perfect for swimming, surfing and all kinds of water sports, and there is a smorgasbord of man-made attractions and entertainment.

The heart of the action is the appropriately named Surfers Paradise, the main town, which offers excellent shopping and dining and a host of nightlife options, including the glossy Jupiters

Casino at nearby Broadbeach. Many of the Gold Coast's attractions are particularly appealing to children, and theme parks like Dreamworld, Warner Bros Movie World, Wet 'n' Wild Water World and the excellent Sea World are extremely popular. There are many fine golf courses in the area, you can take a cruise to tranquil South Stradbroke Island, go water-skiing, or even sample the daredevil sport of bungee jumping. The Coast's list of things to do is almost endless.

If you prefer to stay somewhere quieter, the southern area around Coolangatta offers a less frenetic pace – and fewer high-rise buildings. This is also the location of Currumbin Wildlife Sanctuary. When you've had enough of the coast, a short trip to the hinterland, particularly to Lamington National Park (➤ 113) or the delightful mountain town of Mount Tamborine, is a rewarding experience. Excellent scenery and a cooler environment, with rainforest walking trails and a diversity of art and craft shops, make this town a great day trip.

✚ 24L 🚌 Coach transfers (from Brisbane) 🚆 Gold Coast (from Brisbane) ✈ Coolangatta
ℹ Gold Coast Tourism Bureau ✉ Cavill Avenue, Surfers Paradise ☎ (07) 5538 4419 🕐 Mon–Fri 8.30–5.30, Sat 9–5, Sun 9–3.30

4 Great Barrier Reef, Queensland

www.gbrmpa.gov.au
www.queenslandholidays.com
www.queenslandtravel.com

The Great Barrier Reef is often described as the eighth wonder of the world, and a visit to this marine wonderland will be long remembered.

Running parallel to the Queensland coast for over 2,000km (124 miles) – from Papua New Guinea to just south of the Tropic of Capricorn – the Great Barrier Reef is the world's largest living structure. This extraordinary ecosystem is, in fact, made of over 2,000 linked reefs and around 700 islands and fringing reefs, and is composed of and built by countless tiny coral polyps and algae. This famous natural attraction is protected by its Great Barrier Reef Marine Park status and World Heritage listing.

The reef itself is home to many different types of coral: some are brightly coloured, while others, like the aptly-named staghorns, take on strange formations. The reef's tropical waters host an incredible variety of marine life – everything from tiny, luminously coloured fish to sharks, manta rays, turtles and dolphins. There are many ways to view and explore this fabulous underwater world: scenic

flights, boat trips, snorkelling or scuba diving, and glass-bottom or semi-submersible boat trips are all available.

For the very best Great Barrier Reef experience, it is possible to stay right on the reef. The idyllic coral cays of Green Island, Heron Island and Lady Elliot Island offer resort accommodation, while Lady Musgrave is for campers only. Other options are to base yourself at a coastal resort (Townsville, Cairns and Port Douglas in the north, or the Whitsunday Islands further south are the best bets) or on one of the many non-reef islands. Some island suggestions are Lizard, Dunk and Magnetic Island in the north; Hayman, South Molle and Hamilton in the Whitsunday region; and Great Keppel Island in the south.

➕ 11D 🚂 or ✈ Proserpine, Townsville, Cairns
ℹ Queensland Travel Centre ✉ 30 Makerston Street, Brisbane ☎ (07) 3535 4557 🕐 Mon–Fri 8.30–5

5 Great Ocean Road, Victoria

www.greatoceanrd.org.au

A journey along Australia's most spectacular road reveals superb coastal scenery, charming old resorts and fishing villages, and a forested hinterland.

Extending from Torquay to Port Fairy, Victoria's Great Ocean Road snakes its way along the state's southwest coast for a distance of 300km (185 miles). Geelong, 75km (46 miles) from Melbourne, is a good starting point and nearby Bells Beach, one of Australia's surfing meccas, is a good spot to get in the mood for this oceanside drive.

The quiet village of Anglesea is famous for the kangaroos that roam its local golf course, while Lorne offers fine beaches, a delightful seaside resort atmosphere and forested hillsides inland. Beyond here are the fishing town of Apollo Bay and Otway National Park – an irresistible combination of rugged coastline and lush inland rainforest.

The coast is most dramatic as you reach Port Campbell National Park. The spectacular formations here known as the Twelve Apostles are the result of erosion caused by wind, rain and the stormy Southern Ocean. The picturesque town of Port Campbell is an ideal base for exploring.

Further west along this wild coastline, the aptly named Shipwreck Coast is famous for migrating whales which give birth here between May and August each year. The Great Ocean Road proper ends at the charming fishing village of Port Fairy, where there are over 50 National Trust-listed buildings, beaches and coastal cruises to enjoy.

✚ 21H 🚌 V line: Apollo Bay to Warrnambool, Fri only; driving is the best option 🚍 From Geelong to Warrnambool ❓ Great Ocean Walk: from Apollo Bay to the Twelve Apostles; www.greatoceanwalk.com.au ℹ️ Geelong and Great Ocean Road Visitor Centre ✉️ Princes Highway, Geelong ☎ 1800 620 888 or (03) 5275 5797 🕘 Daily 9–5

6 Kakadu National Park, Northern Territory

www.deh.gov.au/parks/kakadu
www.ntholidays.com

Australia's largest national park is both a superb tropical wilderness and a treasure house of ancient Aboriginal art and culture.

Covering almost 20,000sq km (7,720sq miles) to the east of Darwin, this vast World Heritage-listed national park is one of Australia's most spectacular attractions. Much of Kakadu is a flat, river-crossed floodplain that transforms into a lake during the wet season, but this large area is backed by forested lowlands, hills, and the dramatic 250m (820ft) cliffs of the Arnhem Land escarpment. The extraordinary wildlife within this varied terrain ranges from estuarine crocodiles to dingoes, wallabies, snakes, goannas and over 280 species of birds.

There is much evidence of the area's long Aboriginal occupation, which may have endured for an incredible 50,000 years. Aboriginal-owned Kakadu includes Nourlangie and Ubirr rocks, where you can see fine examples of Aboriginal rock art, estimated to be around 20,000 years old. Among the park's scenic highlights are the spectacular Jim Jim Falls and Twin Falls that tumble off the escarpment, and Yellow Water – a tranquil waterhole and wetlands area, home to prolific birdlife.

During the wet season (November to April) many of the roads are impassable, so the best time to visit Kakadu is during the 'Dry' (May to October). Much of the park can be explored in a normal vehicle, but a four-wheel drive is necessary for off-road travelling. General information is available from Bowali Visitor Centre, but the Warradjan Aboriginal Cultural Centre at Yellow Water provides a deeper insight into the area's Indigenous culture and history. To see something of modern Aboriginal life, you can visit neighbouring Arnhem Land; this is Aboriginal land and permits are required to visit, so a tour is the only real option.

✚ 7E ✋ Moderate 🍴 Cafés in the area ($–$$)
❎ Jabiru ❓ Guided walks from visitor centre
ℹ Bowali Visitor Centre ✉ Kakadu Highway
☎ (08) 8938 1121 🕐 Daily 8–5

7 The Kimberley, Western Australia

www.kimberleytourism.com

In the far north of Western Australia, the Kimberley is one of the continent's remotest and most spectacular regions.

Explored and settled as late as the 1880s, the Kimberley is extremely rugged and very sparsely settled – the population of just 25,000 lives in Aboriginal settlements, on enormous cattle stations, and in a few small towns. This vast region of 420,000sq km (162,120sq miles) is generally divided into two main areas, the West and East Kimberley.

The tropical town of Broome, with its multicultural population, pearling history and fabulous beaches, is the ideal starting point for exploring the western region. The nearby settlement of Derby has an interesting Royal Flying

Doctor Service base, while inland attractions include the dramatic Geikie Gorge National Park, which has a 14km-long gorge.

You can reach the East Kimberley by driving north and east from Broome or flying to Kununurra, a town near the Northern Territory border and the base for the ambitious 1960s and 1970s Ord River Irrigation Scheme. This project created the vast Argyle and Kununurra lakes – welcome breaks in the otherwise arid landscape. From here you can visit the Argyle Diamond Mine, then travel north to the remote port of Wyndham, or south to the wondrous Bungle Bungles. Contained within Purnululu National Park, 'discovered' only in 1983, and given World Heritage status in 2003, these spectacular rock formations, up to 300m (985ft) high, are composed of extremely crumbly silica and sandstone eroded into beehive-like shapes.

Other attractions worth seeing in this wild, last-frontier landscape include the Aboriginal rock art sites of Mirima National Park near Kununurra; Windjana Gorge National Park, reached via the small town of Fitzroy Crossing; and the amazing Wolfe Creek Crater – an enormous depression created by a meteorite.

✚ 5D ✈ Broome or Kununurra ❓ Best visited Apr–Oct. Rental of a four-wheel drive vehicle is recommended. Purnululu National Park closed Jan–Mar
ℹ West Kimberley Tourist Bureau ✉ Corner of Broome Highway and Bagot Road, Broome; East Kimberley Tourist Bureau ✉ Coolibah Drive, Kununurra; Broome Tourist Bureau ☎ (08) 9192 2222; Kununurra Tourist Bureau ☎ (08) 9168 1177 🕐 Daily, generally 9–4

8 Sydney Harbour and Sydney Opera House

www.sydneyoperahouse.com

Complemented by the ethereal, sail-like outlines of the famous Opera House, Sydney Harbour is the glittering jewel of Australia's most famous city.

From the day in January 1788 when the 11 convict-bearing ships of the First Fleet sailed into Port Jackson, Sydney's harbour has been the focus of this great city. A harbour cruise – be it on a luxury

boat or a humble Sydney ferry – is a must. From the water you will see the city, including the large areas of the Sydney Harbour National Park, from a new perspective. Ferries are also the best way to reach waterfront suburbs and the harbour's beaches. From Circular Quay you can take a trip to the beaches of Manly on the north side of the harbour, or to the southside suburb of Watsons Bay, close to the harbour's entrance. Ferries also visit some of the national park's islands, including historic Fort Denison.

On the harbour's southern shore, the curved roofs of the Sydney Opera House soar above Bennelong Point. Completed in 1973, after 14 years and many technical and political problems, this architectural masterpiece, designed by Danish architect Joern Utzon, still inspires controversy. However, there is no doubt that the structure's stone platform and dramatic white roofs, covered with over a million ceramic tiles, have made it one of the world's most distinctive buildings. Once you have inspected the exterior, attending a performance or taking a guided tour of the five performance halls is highly recommended. Above the magnificent harbour is the third ingredient of this classic Sydney scene: the Sydney Harbour Bridge (➤ 85), completed in 1932 and, with a tunnel running underground, still the major link between the south and north shores.

🚩 *Sydney 4h* ✉ Opera House: Bennelong Point
☎ Performance details (02) 9250 7777; tours: (02) 9250 7250;
www.sydneyoperahouse.com 💷 Moderate–Expensive
🍴 Guillaume at Bennelong restaurant ($$$), cafés ($–$$)
🚢 Circular Quay ❓ Guided tours 8.30–5. Performances include opera, ballet, classical music and theatre

9 Tasmania's World Heritage Area

www.park.tas.gov.au

Much of Tasmania is superb wilderness, and the island's relatively small size makes these untouched areas easily accessible.

Tasmania's wilderness is of such significant natural beauty that around 20 per cent – an incredible 1.38 million hectares (3.4 million acres) – of the state is under World Heritage protection. This land of rugged peaks, wild rivers, moorland and remote coastline also contains many sites of Aboriginal significance, while the wildlife includes Tasmanian devils, echidnas and the elusive platypus.

One of the most accessible regions in the World Heritage Area is the Cradle Mountain-Lake St Clair National Park, just 170km (105 miles) from the capital, Hobart. The alpine scenery here is truly spectacular – including high peaks such as Mount Ossa (1,617m/5,305ft), as well as the state's highest mountain, lakes, alpine moorlands and rainforests. There are many hiking trails here, the most famous of which is the five-to ten-day Overland Track in the heart of the Cradle Mountain-Lake St Clair National Park.

To the south, the Franklin-Gordon Wild Rivers National Park is particularly famous for its adventurous Franklin

River whitewater rafting. Even more remote and untamed wilderness is found in the Southwest National Park, the domain of forests, lakes and a long, deeply indented coastline. Experienced hikers will enjoy the challenge of this park's 85km (53-mile) South Coast Track. Much closer to Hobart and characterized by its heathlands and rugged dolerite ranges, is the Hartz Mountains National Park.

November to April are the best months to explore these areas, but the weather can be unpredictable at any time, changing in minutes from warm and sunny to rain, or even snow.

➕ 21G 🅿️ Parks: inexpensive 🚌 From Hobart, Devonport and Launceston to some locations; driving is the best option ❌ Southwest National Park ℹ️ Tasmanian Parks and Wildlife Service ✉️ 134 Macquarie Street, Hobart ☎️ 1300 135 513 or (03) 6233 6191 🕐 Mon–Fri 9–5

10 Uluru-Kata Tjuta National Park, Northern Territory

www.deh.gov.au/parks/uluru/
www.centralaustraliantourism.com

This 1,325ha (3,275-acre) World Heritage Site incorporates two of Australia's most spectacular sights – Uluru (Ayers Rock) and neighbouring Kata Tjuta (The Olgas).

Located at the centre of the continent, Uluru's vast bulk is an extraordinary and overwhelming sight. At 348m (1,142ft) high and with a base circumference of some 9km (5.5 miles), this is the world's largest monolith – a massive rock which is made even more dramatic by its setting on the monotonous plains of the Red Centre. Uluru was first sighted by Europeans in 1872, but this area has been sacred to the local Anangu people for tens of thousands of years. It is possible to climb Uluru, but the activity is discouraged by the Anangu landowners as the rock is a sacred site; under traditional law, climbing is prohibited to everyone except senior men initiated into Anangu culture. The climb can also be dangerous; 37 people have died attempting to ascend the monolith and many have been injured. Other options are to take a hiking tour of the base, and to view Uluru at sunset, when its normally dark red colour changes dramatically as the light fades.

Although, like Uluṟu, it is the tip of a vast underground formation, Kata Tjuṯa, 30km (18 miles) to the west, offers a rather different experience. The name means 'many heads' – an appropriate description of the 30 or so massive rocks which make up Kata Tjuṯa. The domes are sacred and are strictly off limits to visitors. Access is permitted on the established walking trails, but most of these should be undertaken only if you are well prepared.

A visit to the Uluṟu-Kata Tjuṯa Cultural Centre, just 1km (0.5 miles) from Uluṟu, is a must. This excellent complex includes displays on Aboriginal culture and history, demonstrations of traditional art and dance, and a shop that sells local arts and crafts. The base for exploring the national park is the well-designed Ayers Rock Resort village.

✚ 6B 👖 Expensive ⊙ Dec–Feb daily 5–9; Mar 5.30–8.30; Apr 6–8; May 6–7.30; Jun–Jul 6.30–7.30; Aug 6–7.30; Sep 5.30–7:30; Oct 5–8; Nov 5–8.30 (parts of the park may be temporarily closed for cultural reasons) ✖ Connellan airport ℹ Cultural centre ☎ (08) 8956 1128 ⊙ Daily 7–6

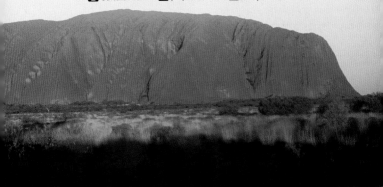

Best things to do

Ways to be a local

Relax, Australia is not the place to go in for excessive formality, and 'no worries' is not a popular expression for nothing.

Use 'g'day' instead of 'hello'.

Dress casually – summer shorts and sandals are acceptable in nearly all places.

Go to a cricket match, or an Aussie Rules football game in winter, to soak up the atmosphere of the national sports.

Get invited to an Aussie barbecue, where you will enjoy a relaxed meal and a unique cultural experience.

Wear a hat, not just for fashion, but as a necessity to avoid the sun's harmful rays.

Head for an Aussie pub or two to sample the excellent local beers and wines.

Learn the basic facts about convict, colonial and Aboriginal history, and remember that racist jokes are in extremely bad taste.

Spend most of your time outdoors, particularly on the beach or bushwalking.

Good places to have lunch

Arintji ($$)

An excellent café in the heart of the Federation Square precinct.
✉ Federation Square, Melbourne ☎ (03) 9663 9900 ⏰ Lunch and dinner
daily 🚋 City Circle tram

City Gardens Café ($–$$)

A delightful café set in Brisbane's lush Botanic Gardens.
✉ City Botanic Gardens, Alice Street, Brisbane ☎ (07) 3229 1554;
www.citygardens.com.au ⏰ Breakfast, lunch and afternoon tea 🚌 The Loop

Doyle's on the Beach ($$$)
Sydney's most famous seafood restaurant right on the water.
✉ 11 Marine Parade, Watsons Bay, Sydney ☎ (02) 9337 2007;
www.doyles.com.au ⊕ Lunch and dinner daily 🚌 324, 325

Fraser's ($$–$$$)
Modern Australian dining in Perth's parklands.
✉ Fraser Avenue, Kings Park, West Perth ☎ (08) 9481 7100;
www.frasersrestaurant.com.au ⊕ Breakfast, lunch and dinner daily 🚌 33

Jolleys Boathouse ($$)
Modern Australian food in a delightful setting on the Torrens River.
✉ Jolleys Lane, Adelaide ☎ (08) 8223 2891; www.jolleysboathouse.com
⊕ Lunch Sun–Fri, dinner Mon–Sat

Juniperberry ($$)
Modern Australian cuisine served in the gallery's sculpture garden.
✉ National Gallery of Australia, Parkes, Canberra ☎ (02) 6240 6665
⊕ Lunch daily 🚌 34

Mures Upper Deck ($$–$$$)
A great seafood menu in the perfect waterfront spot.
✉ Mures Fish Centre, Victoria Dock, Hobart ☎ (03) 6231 1999;
www.mures.com.au ⊕ Lunch and dinner daily

Nudel Bar ($)
Good-value noodle and pasta dishes from all over the world.
✉ 76 Bourke Street, Melbourne ☎ (03) 9662 9100 ⊕ Lunch and dinner daily
🚌 City Circle tram

Pee Wee's at the Point ($$–$$$)
On the Darwin beachfront. Modern Australian cuisine.
✉ Alec Fong Lim Drive, East Point, Darwin ☎ (08) 8981 6868;
www.peewees.com.au

Top activities

Boating: sail a yacht around Queensland's Whitsunday Islands, or rent a houseboat on the Murray River.

Bushwalking: there are countless places to go hiking, but try Tasmania (➤ 52–53) and the Blue Mountains (➤ 36–37).

Cross-country skiing: the conditions are ideal around the ski fields of Victoria, Tasmania and New South Wales (Jun–Oct).

Fishing: from trout fishing in Tasmania's lakes to big-game marlin wrestling off Cairns.

Four-wheel-driving adventures: the Pinnacles in WA is an ideal venue.

Golf: in Australia golf is a sport for everyone. There are excellent courses everywhere, but those on the Gold Coast are particularly recommended.

Horse riding: the southeast is ideal – around the Snowy Mountains of NSW and Victoria's alpine areas.

Scuba diving and snorkelling: there is nowhere better than along the Great Barrier Reef.

Surfing: the quintessential Aussie sport – Sydney's coastline, Bells Beach in Victoria and the Margaret River in Western Australia are all good spots.

Tennis: you will find day/night courts in every major city.

Great views

- From Cottesloe Beach at sunset, Perth.

- From Echo Point in the Blue Mountains, Katoomba.

- From Kings Park over the Swan River and city, Perth.

- From Melbourne Observation Deck, Melbourne.

- From Mount Coot-tha, Brisbane.

- From Mount Wellington, Hobart.
- From the Sydney Tower or Skywalk, Sydney.
- From the top of the Sydney Harbour Bridge, Sydney.
- From Telstra Tower on Black Mountain, Canberra.
- Uluru at dawn or dusk, Uluru-Kata Tjuta National Park.

Exceptional lesser-known destinations

● **Bathurst and Melville islands, Northern Territory:** the home of the Indigenous Tiwi people and their traditional culture.

● **Bunbury, Western Australia:** swim with wild dolphins at the Dolphin Discovery Centre here.

● **Coober Pedy, South Australia:** an opal mining town with most buildings underground.

● **Jervis Bay, New South Wales:** white sands, clear blue waters and unspoiled bushland.

● **Ningaloo Reef, near Exmouth, Western Australia:** the diving here rivals that of the Great Barrier Reef.

● **Norfolk Island:** an external territory of Australia, packed with fascinating convict and colonial history.

● **Phillip Island, Victoria:** gourmet food and fairy penguins.

Good places to stay

NEW SOUTH WALES AND THE
AUSTRALIAN CAPITAL TERRITORY
Canberra Rex ($–$$)
Conveniently located within easy walking distance of the city.
✉ 150 Northbourne Ave, Braddon, Canberra ☎ (02) 6248 5311;
www.canberrarexhotel.com.au

Quay Grand Suites ($$$)
In a magnificent location right on Circular Quay, a stone's throw
from the Opera House, Harbour Bridge and Botanic Gardens.
✉ 61 Macquarie Street, East Circular Quay, Sydney ☎ (02) 9256 4000

Carlton Crest ($$)
Elegant rooms overlooking Darling Harbour and close to the
entertainment district.
✉ 169–179 Thomas Street, Sydney ☎ (02) 9281 6888;
www.carltoncrest-sydney.com.au

Peppers Convent ($$$)
One of the Hunter Valley's best hotels, the historic Convent
provides spacious rooms that open onto a veranda.
✉ Halls Road, Pokolbin, Hunter Valley ☎ (02) 4998 7764;
www.peppers.com.au

QUEENSLAND
Hotel Ibis ($$)
Close to the Brisbane River and within walking distance of major
tourist attractions.
✉ 27–35 Turbot Street, Brisbane ☎ (07) 3237 2333

Reef Palms ($–$$$)
Traditional Queenslander-style accommodation close to The
Esplanade, with a range of room types.
✉ 41 Digger St, Cairns ☎ (07) 4051 2599; www.reefpalms.com.au

VICTORIA
Sheraton Towers Southgate ($$$)
One of Melbourne's best hotels, this modern establishment rises above the Southgate dining, arts and leisure precinct.
✉ 1 Southgate Avenue, Southbank ☎ (03) 8696 8888;

Victoria Hotel ($–$$)
A grand, historic hotel in the heart of Melbourne. Very good value.
✉ 215 Little Collins Street, Melbourne ☎ (03) 9653 0441;
www.victoriahotel.com.au 🚋 Any Swanston Walk tram

TASMANIA
Somerset on the Pier ($$$)
A luxurious hotel with loft-style bedrooms. The waterfront setting, on a 1930s pier, is superb.
✉ Elizabeth Street Pier, Hobart ☎ (03) 6220 6600; www.the-ascott.com

SOUTH AUSTRALIA
Quest Mansions ($–$$)
Spacious self-contained apartments in an historic building close to all the main attractions.
✉ 21 Pulteney Street, Adelaide ☎ (08) 8232 0033;
www.questmansions.com.au 🚌 City Loop

NORTHERN TERRITORY
Holiday Inn Esplanade Darwin ($$–$$$)
One of Darwin's best hotels, with a restaurant and sports facilities.
✉ 122 The Esplanade, Darwin ☎ (08) 8980 0800; www.ichotelsgroup.com

WESTERN AUSTRALIA
Riverview on Mount St ($$)
Self-contained studio apartments. Close to city and Kings Park.
✉ 42 Mount Street, Perth ☎ (08) 9321 8963; www.riverview.com.au

Places to take the children

NEW SOUTH WALES
Scenic World
Scenic Railway and Sceniscender rides deep into the valley, as well as walking tracks, wildlife and a forest boardwalk.
✉ Corner Violet Street and Cliff Drive, Katoomba, Blue Mountains
☎ (02) 4782 2699 🕐 Daily 9–5 🚆 Katoomba

Western Plains Zoo
Slightly off the beaten path (five hours' drive from Sydney), this excellent open-range zoo has over a thousand animals in enclosures replicating the animals' natural habitats. Bicycle rental and barbecue facilities make it fun day out for the family.
✉ Obley Rd, Dubbo ☎ (02) 6881 1400 🕐 Daily 9–5 🚆 or ✈ Dubbo

QUEENSLAND
Australian Woolshed
Just 20 minutes from Brisbane, you can watch sheep and sheepdog shows and visit the wildlife park.
✉ 148 Samford Road, Ferny Hills, Brisbane ☎ (07) 3872 1100 🕐 Daily 9–5
🚆 Ferny Grove

Tjapukai Aboriginal Cultural Park
North of Cairns, this exciting and educational complex includes dance shows, boomerang throwing, an Aboriginal camp and other aspects of Indigenous culture.
✉ Kamerunga Road, Smithfield, Cairns ☎ (07) 4042 9900 🕐 Daily 9–5 and some evenings 🚌 Marlin Coast Sun Bus

VICTORIA
Scienceworks
A suburban Melbourne museum with fun, hands-on exhibits, live science shows and technological activities.
✉ 2 Booker Street, Spotswood, Melbourne ☎ (03) 9392 4800 🕐 Daily 10–4.30. Closed Good Fri, 25 Dec 🚆 Spotswood

TASMANIA
Bonorong Wildlife Park
A wildlife park near Hobart, where you can meet Tasmanian devils, wombats, koalas, kangaroos and other native animals.

✉ Briggs Road, Brighton ☎ (03) 6268 1184 🕐 Daily 9–5. Closed 25 Dec
🚌 Tasmanian Redline bus from Hobart

Cadbury Chocolate Factory
Taking children on a tour of this tempting attraction near Hobart may be asking for trouble, but it's a fun experience. Reservations essential. Children must have adult supervision.

✉ Cadbury Road, Claremont, Hobart ☎ (03) 6249 0333 🕐 Mon–Fri: tours from 8–3. Closed all public hols 🚢 or 🚌 From Hobart

SOUTH AUSTRALIA
South Australian Migration Museum
The story of immigration to culturally diverse South Australia, with interactive and educational activities for children.

✉ 82 Kintore Avenue, Adelaide ☎ (08) 8207 7580 🕐 Mon–Fri 10–5, Sat–Sun 1–5

NORTHERN TERRITORY
Aquascene
Every day at high tide, thousands of fish come here to be hand fed – an experience that should appeal to children.

✉ 28 Doctors Gully Road, Darwin ☎ (08) 8981 7837 🕐 Daily. Feeding times depend on tides

WESTERN AUSTRALIA
Rottnest Island
Children will enjoy the sandy beaches, clear waters and cute quokkas – small marsupials that roam the island (▶ 180).

✉ Rottnest Island Visitor Centre, Thomson Bay ☎ (08) 9372 9752
🕐 Daily 8.30–5

Arts, crafts and souvenirs

ABORIGINAL ART AND CRAFT

Aboriginal Art Galleries of Australia

Specializing in Aboriginal artworks from the Central Desert region.

✉ 35 Spring Street, Melbourne ☎ (03) 9654 2516

Gavala Aboriginal Cultural Centre

Sydney outlet specializing in Indigenous art, music and souvenirs.

✉ Shop 377, Harbourside, Darling Harbour, Sydney ☎ (02) 9212 7232

Papunya Tula Artists

A gallery owned and directed by Aboriginal people from the Western Desert, selling quality artworks from the region.

✉ 63 Todd Mall, Alice Springs ☎ (08) 8952 4731; www.papunyatula.com.au

Queensland Aboriginal Creations

A range of Indigenous items, from didgeridoos to woodcarvings.

✉ 199 Elizabeth Street, Brisbane ☎ (07) 3224 5730

Tandanya Aboriginal Cultural Institute
This centre's giftshop is stocked with well-made Aboriginal artworks and artefacts.
✉ 253 Grenfell Street, Adelaide ☎ (08) 8224 3200

AUSTRALIANA
Australian Choice
This shop sells quality Australian-made products, great for gifts and souvenirs.
✉ Canberra Centre, Bunda Street, Canberra City ☎ (02) 6257 5315

Body Map
A wide range of Australian-made products and souvenirs.
✉ Shop 156A, Melbourne Central and 211 La Trobe Street, Melbourne
☎ (03) 9662 2900

Done Art & Design
Ken Done's colourful Australian designs, printed on beachwear, accessories and housewares.
✉ 123 George Street, The Rocks, Sydney ☎ (02) 9251 6099

Naturally Tasmanian
One of Hobart's best souvenir shops, selling Aussie clothing, sheepskin products, local foodstuffs and much more.
✉ 59 Salamanca Place, Hobart ☎ (03) 6223 4248

RM Williams
The original 'Bushman's Outfitters', where you can buy Akubra hats, Drizabone oilskin coats and country-style clothing.
✉ 389 George Street, Sydney ☎ (02) 9262 2228

South Australian Museum
Museum shop, good for unusual Australian gifts and souvenirs.
✉ North Terrace, Adelaide ☎ (08) 8207 7500 🚍 City Loop

a walk

around Sydney Opera House, the Botanic Gardens and Macquarie Street

Stroll around the harbour foreshore, visit historic buildings and explore the Art Gallery of NSW.

Start at Circular Quay.

Lively Circular Quay is the focus of the city's ferry system. There are many cafés and street entertainers in the area.

Follow the Circular Quay East walkway towards the Opera House (➤ 50–51).

Take in the exterior of Australia's most famous building, then explore the performance halls in a guided tour.

Enter the Botanic Gardens via the gate near the Opera House.

Sydney's waterfront Royal Botanic Gardens contain an outstanding collection of native and imported flora. The lush Sydney Tropical Centre is a highlight here.

After exploring the gardens, continue around the foreshore to the eastern side of the cove.

From Mrs Macquaries Point there are classic views of Sydney Harbour, the Opera House and the Harbour Bridge.

Head south along Mrs Macquaries Road until you reach the Art Gallery.

The Art Gallery of New South Wales is the state's premier gallery, with superb examples of Australian, Aboriginal, European and Asian art. By the gallery is the Domain, a large parkland area.

Follow Art Gallery Road until you reach College Street, then turn right.

Gracious Macquarie Street contains many historic buildings, including the 1819 Hyde Park Barracks, once a home for convicts but now a fascinating museum, and State Parliament House, dating from 1816.

Continue along Macquarie Street, then turn left into Albert Street to return to Circular Quay.

Distance 3km (2 miles)
Time 2–4 hours, depending on Opera House and museum visits
Start/end point Circular Quay ✚ *Sydney 3f* 🚇 Circular Quay
Lunch Botanic Gardens Restaurant and Kiosk ($–$$) ✉ Royal Botanic Gardens ☎ (02) 9241 2419

Markets

SYDNEY, NEW SOUTH WALES
Glebe Market
A bohemian Saturday market brimming with clothing, music, jewellery and food, best enjoyed in a sunny spot on the grass.
✉ Glebe Public School, 183 Glebe Point Road ⏰ Sat 10–4
☎ (02) 4237 7499 🚌 370, 431, 432, 433

Paddington Markets
A vibrant market with over 250 stalls selling clothes, arts and crafts. Good food and free entertainment.
✉ 395 Oxford Street, Paddington ☎ (02) 9331 2923 ⏰ Sat 10–4 🚌 378, 380, L82

The Rocks Market
Arts, crafts, jewellery and housewares in the heart of Sydney's tourist mecca.
✉ Upper George Street, The Rocks ☎ (02) 9240 8717 ⏰ Sat–Sun 10–5 🚆 Circular Quay

CANBERRA, AUSTRALIAN CAPITAL TERRITORY
Old Bus Depot Markets
On Sundays, this old Canberra bus depot is transformed into a covered market. Hand-made goods and collectables are the main items for sale.
✉ 49 Wentworth Avenue, Kingston ☎ (02) 6292 8391 ⏰ Sun 10–4, also Sat in December 🚌 39

BRISBANE, QUEENSLAND
Eagle Street Pier Craft Market
A Sunday city-centre market offering quality handcrafted goods such as clothes, arts and crafts and some great gifts.
✉ Riverside Centre and Eagle Street Pier, Eagle Street ⏰ Sun 8–3
☎ (07) 3846 4500 🚌 The Loop

MELBOURNE, VICTORIA
Queen Victoria Market
This Melbourne institution is a large indoor market selling everything from foodstuffs to fashion clothing.
✉ Corner Elizabeth and Victoria Streets ☎ (03) 9320 5822 🕐 Daily except Mon 🚊 Tram 19, 57, 59

St Kilda Esplanade Art and Craft Market
Popular market with over 200 stalls selling hand-crafted items.
✉ The Esplanade, St Kilda ☎ (03) 9209 6666 🕐 Sun 10–5 🚊 St Kilda tram

HOBART, TASMANIA
Salamanca Market
The place to be in Hobart on Saturdays – an excellent market, set against the historic backdrop of Salamanca Place.
✉ Salamanca Place ☎ (03) 6238 2843 🕐 Sat 8.30–3 🚊 None

ADELAIDE, SOUTH AUSTRALIA
Central Market
Dating from 1870, this is mainly a produce market – but a fascinating place to wander around nonetheless.
✉ Grote and Gouger Streets ☎ (08) 8203 7495 🕐 Tue, Thu–Sat. Closed public holidays 🚊 City Loop

DARWIN, NORTHERN TERRITORY
Mindil Beach Sunset Markets
An evening market with arts, crafts, food and free entertainment.
✉ Mindil Beach 🕐 May–Oct, Thu and Sun 🚊 None

FREMANTLE, WESTERN AUSTRALIA
Fremantle Markets
A National Trust-classified indoor market that sells fresh produce, clothing and crafts.
✉ 84 South Terrace, Fremantle ☎ (08) 9335 2515 🕐 Fri–Sun 🚊 Fremantle

Exploring

Australia is a young nation in an ancient land. Its people are from diverse backgrounds; some have been here for more than 60,000 years, but many – a third of the popuation – have arrived in only the last 60. Although proud of its pioneering history and Outback traditions, this is the world's most urbanised society, with 88 per cent of people living in towns and cities.

The Australian landscape varies greatly, encompassing lush tropical rainforests, an arid desert interior, snowy peaks and sandy beaches; but wherever you go, the scenery is spectacular, the atmosphere is laid back and the sun is likely to be shining.

New South Wales and the Australian Capital Territory

New South Wales, named by Cook in 1770 because it reminded him of south Wales, is Australia's fourth-largest state but has the largest population – almost 6.7 million. Geographically, it is made up of a series of parallel strips: a narrow coastal plain which supports the bulk of the population, the uplands of the Great Dividing Range, slopes and plains which form the state's agricultural heartland and, finally, the Outback. The climate varies from subtropical in the north to the winter snows of the mountains in the far south.

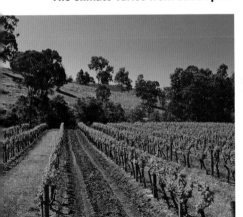

Although within the boundaries of New South Wales, the Australian Capital Territory, or ACT, is governed and administered separately. The territory and the national capital, Canberra, were created early in the 20th century to resolve the long-running rivalry between Sydney and Melbourne over which city should be the nation's capital.

www.visitnsw.com.au

Sydney

The nation's birthplace has developed from its humble convict beginnings into a vibrant metropolis that holds its own on the world stage. With a multicultural population of over 4 million, Sydney is the continent's largest and, many would say, most brash, city. Although the pace of life is faster here than anywhere else in Australia, Sydneysiders still know how to relax – the city's harbour, long golden beaches and surrounding bushland make sure of that.

In recent years Sydney has truly come of age as a major city and an enviable tourist destination. It has been voted 'the world's best city' by discerning travellers the world over, but perhaps the biggest accolade of all came when Sydney was chosen as the host city for the 2000 Summer Olympic Games. In addition to the fascinating convict history, museums, galleries and, of course, the 'Great Outdoors', the city offers wonderful shopping, an innovative and highly acclaimed restaurant scene and a wide choice of nightlife.

Although visitors spend most of their time in the inner city and eastern suburbs, an entirely different world lies beyond. To the north lie the glorious Northern Beaches with surf, sand and a far more relaxed lifestyle, the charming waterway of Pittwater, and the bushland of Ku-ring-gai Chase National Park. To the west, you can visit historic Parramatta and Sydney Olympic Park, the Olympic Games site. Sydney's inner suburbs also have a great deal to offer. A visit to famous Bondi, Manly or one of the many other beaches is a must.

www.seesydney.com.au

✚ 23K

AUSTRALIAN MUSEUM

A world-class natural history museum, this is an excellent place to learn about pre-European Aboriginal life and Australia's native fauna. Also featured are human evolution, minerals, dinosaurs, biodiversity and a fascinating skeletons room.

www.austmus.gov.au

✚ *Sydney 4c* ✉ 6 College Street ☎ (02) 9320 6000 🕐 Daily 9.30–5. Closed 25 Dec 👷 Moderate

DARLING HARBOUR

With its harbourside shopping and eating complexes, the delightful Chinese Garden, the Imax Theatre and National Maritime Museum, Darling Harbour is one of Sydney's most popular recreation areas. One of the best attractions here is the **Sydney Aquarium,** where you will encounter sharks, crocodiles and colourful Great Barrier Reef fish at close quarters. The nearby

futuristic building of the Australian National Maritime Museum contains several galleries covering maritime themes as diverse as the discovery of Australia and surfboard technology. Many of the exhibits are interactive. Moored outside are various vessels, including a World War II destroyer and a submarine.

www.darlingharbour.com

✚ *Sydney 2c* ✉ Darling Harbour
☎ (02) 9240 8500 🕐 Daily 9.30–5.30

Sydney Aquarium

☎ (02) 8751 7800 🕐 Daily 9am –10pm (last admission at 9)
👷 Expensive 🚝 Monorail Darling Park

POWERHOUSE MUSEUM

Sydney's largest museum is an entertaining technological and cultural wonderland with everything from a huge 18th-century steam engine and a 1930s art deco cinema to holograms and irresistible hands-on computer displays.

www.phm.gov.au

🔲 *Sydney 2b* ✉ 500 Harris Street, Ultimo ☎ (02) 9217 0111 🕐 Daily 10–5. Closed 25 Dec ✋ Moderate

THE ROCKS

With its intriguing past and prime harbourside location, this is Sydney's tourist mecca. It was the site of Australia's first 'village' and has had a colourful history. In addition to wandering the narrow streets, sitting on the waterfront and browsing in the many shops, Rocks highlights are a lively weekend market and several small museums – including the Sydney Observatory at nearby Millers Point. Full details of the area are available from the Information Centre.

www.sydneyvisitorcentre.com

 *Sydney 3g* 🚇 Circular Quay
ℹ️ Sydney Visitor Centre ✉️ Corner of Argyle and
Playfair streets, The Rocks ☎ (02) 9240 8788
🕐 Daily 9.30–5.30. Closed 25 Dec, Good Fri

SYDNEY HARBOUR
See pages 50–51.

SYDNEY HARBOUR BRIDGE
Completed in 1932, this famous bridge is still
the primary link between the harbour's north
and south shores, although the Sydney Harbour
Tunnel now handles a large share of the traffic.
You can inspect the bridge from close up by
taking the walkway from the Rocks, and then
climbing the 200 steps of the Pylon. For really
spectacular views of the harbour and city, take
the BridgeClimb tour.
Sydney 3h ☎ Pylon Lookout: (02) 9247 3408;
BridgeClimb: (02) 8274 7777; www.bridgeclimb.com
🕐 Lookout and Museum: daily 10–5. Closed 25 Dec
💰 Lookout: inexpensive; BridgeClimb: expensive
🚇 Circular Quay

SYDNEY OPERA HOUSE

See pages 50–51.

SYDNEY TOWER

The best view in town is from the top of this 304.8m (1,000ft) tower. From the observation level there are superb 360-degree views of the city and its surroundings. The tower has two revolving restaurants; particularly spectacular at night. The more adventurous might like to try the Skywalk, which involves being harnessed to the edge of a moving, glass-floored platform outside the tower for 90 minutes.

✚ *Sydney 3d* ✉ 100 Market Street ☎ (02) 9333 9222; www.skywalk.com.au 🕐 Tower: Sun–Fri 9–10.30, Sat 9 –11.30. Skywalk: daily 9–10 (last skywalk 8.15pm)

TARONGA ZOO

Reached by a scenic ferry ride, Taronga is visited as much for its harbourside location as for the opportunity to meet native Australian wildlife. There are koalas, kangaroos, echidnas, wombats and Tasmanian devils here, as well as native birds and reptiles, and a large collection of other zoo animals.

www.zoo.nsw.gov.au

✚ *Sydney 3d (off map)* ✉ Bradleys Head Road, Mosman ☎ (02) 9969 2777 🕐 Daily 9–5 ✋ Expensive 🍴 Cafés ($$) and kiosk ($) 🚌 247 ⛴ From Circular Quay

Canberra and the Australian Capital Territory (ACT)

Created out of New South Wales farmland after its site was designated in 1908, Canberra is a planned city unlike anywhere else in the nation. Designed by American architect Walter Burley Griffin, and surrounded by parks and gardens, the national capital is a pleasant environment. Canberra is the home of Australia's Federal government; 40 per cent of the 321,000 population is employed in this field. The city is full of diplomatic missions and government departments, and – appealing for the visitor – national museums and galleries. The central focus is man-made Lake Burley Griffin, a location for cruises, from where roads radiate to suburbs and wild bushland. Beyond the city, the surrounding Australian Capital Territory offers rugged Namadgi National Park, Tidbinbilla Nature Reserve and 1859 Lanyon Homestead.

www.canberratourism.com.au ✚ 22J

AUSTRALIAN NATIONAL BOTANIC GARDENS

Containing the world's best collection of unique Australian flora, these gardens feature more than 600 species of eucalyptus trees, a rock garden, the delightful rainforest gully, and a Tasmanian alpine garden. Self-guided arrow trails make it easy to find your way around.

Looming behind the gardens is Black Mountain (779m/2,555ft), capped by the futuristic Telstra Tower. There is a spectacular view of the city and surrounds from the tower's viewing gallery.

www.anbg.gov.au

✉ Clunies Ross Street, Acton ☎ (02) 6250 9540 🕙 Feb–Dec daily 8.30–5; Jan Mon–Fri 8.30–6, Sat–Sun 8.30–8. Closed 25 Dec 💲 Free 🍴 Café ($–$$) 🚌 34 to University then 10-minute walk ❓ Free tours

AUSTRALIAN WAR MEMORIAL

In a dramatic location at the head of Anzac Parade, this impressive monument and museum commemorates the Australians who served in various wars. Its many thousands of displays include aeroplanes, tanks, guns, military memorabilia and artworks.

www.awm.gov.au

✉ Treloar Crescent, Campbell ☎ (02) 6243 4211 🕙 Daily 10–5 💲 Free 🍴 Cafés ($–$$) 🚌 33

NATIONAL GALLERY OF AUSTRALIA

This is the nation's premier gallery, and the ideal place to view good examples of Aboriginal and Australian art. European, Asian and American artworks are also featured, and the gallery hosts excellent travelling exhibitions.

www.nga.gov.au

✉ Parkes Place, Parkes ☎ (02) 6240 6502 🕐 Daily 10–5. Closed Good Fri, 25 Dec ✋ Free

NATIONAL MUSEUM OF AUSTRALIA

Opened in 2001, this modern museum explores the key issues, events and people that have shaped Australia. The themed galleries employ state-of-the-art technology and feature the symbols of the nation, indigenous peoples, and stories of ordinary and famous Australians.

www.nma.gov.au

✉ Lawson Crescent, Acton Peninsula ☎ (02) 6208 5000 🕐 Daily 9–5 ✋ Free general entry 🚌 34

PARLIAMENT HOUSE

Canberra's architectural and political centrepiece was completed in 1988, at a staggering cost of over $1,000 million. It contains the House of Representatives and the Senate, and features fine artworks and craftsmanship. Guided tours are available, and the view from the roof is superb. Also in this Parliamentary Triangle area stands the more modest 1927 Old Parliament House, now housing the National Portrait Gallery.

www.aph.gov.au

✉ Capital Hill ☎ (02) 6277 7111 🕐 Daily 9–5 (later when Parliament is sitting). Closed 25 Dec

🤚 Free 🍴 Café ($–$$) 🚌 31, 34, 39
❓ Guided tours every 20 mins. Book for
Question Time (☎ (02) 6277 4889)

QUESTACON

Also known as The National
Science and Technology Centre,
this exciting, modern complex
brings the world of science alive.
Education and entertainment are
combined brilliantly in the 170 or
so interactive exhibits.

www.questacon.edu.au

✉ King Edward Terrace, Parkes ☎ (02)
6270 2800 🕐 Daily 9–5 🤚 Moderate

What to See in New South Wales

BLUE MOUNTAINS
See pages 36–37.

BROKEN HILL
Broken Hill's harsh landscape is far removed from the waterside ambience of Sydney. This silver-mining town in far western NSW is a good Outback destination. Here you can tour one of the mines, visit the Royal Flying Doctor Service base, and take a trip to nearby Kinchega National Park or the ghost town of Silverton.

www.visitbrokenhill.com.au

✚ 20K 🚂 or ✈ From Sydney 🛈 Broken Hill Visitor Centre ✉ Blende Street ☎ (08) 8087 6077 ⏰ Daily 8.30–5

BYRON BAY
With a wonderful climate, sandy beaches and pounding surf, 'Byron' attracts surfers, scuba divers and holidaymakers in droves. Walk to Cape Byron (Australia's most easterly point), enjoy fine restaurants, or just browse the art and craft shops. Take a drive to the hinterland rainforests or the nearby town of Mullumbimby.

www.visitbyronbay.com

✚ 24L ✈ Ballina or Lismore, then a drive 🛈 Byron Bay Visitor Centre ✉ 80 Jonson Street ☎ (02) 6680 8558 ⏰ Daily 9–5

COFFS HARBOUR
Tourism and banana growing are the main industries of this coastal city, which offers excellent beaches and a sunny climate. Kids will enjoy the Pet Porpoise Pool and Big Banana leisure park, while a drive inland to the picturesque town of Bellingen and rainforests of World Heritage-listed Dorrigo National Park is recommended.

www.visitcoffsharbour.com

✚ 24L 🚂 or ✈ From Sydney 🛈 Coffs Coast Visitor Centre ✉ Corner Pacific Highway and Maclean streets ☎ 1300 369 070 or (02) 6652 1522 ⏰ Daily 9–5

a drive in the Blue Mountains

Explore one of Sydney's favourite recreation areas: the rugged and scenic Blue Mountains.

From central Sydney, go west (towards the Olympic Park) along Parramatta Road, to join the Western Motorway (M4). Continue on to the Great Western Highway (Route 32) at the base of the mountains.

After Glenbrook (information centre), continue to the Norman Lindsay Gallery and Museum at Faulconbridge, devoted to one of Australia's most celebrated artists and writers. Wentworth Falls offers short bushwalks and the Falls Reserve.

Continue on the highway until you reach the Leura turnoff (approximately 2 hours' drive from Sydney).

The picturesque town of Leura has cafés, crafts shops and the historic Everglades Gardens.

Take the signposted scenic Cliff Drive to nearby Katoomba.

This brings you to Echo Point with spectacular views of the Three Sisters, the surrounding cliffs, and the forested Jamison Valley.

Continue on the Cliff Drive, which rejoins the Great Western Highway. Follow the signs to Blackheath.

In Blackheath, head for the National Parks and Wildlife Service Heritage Centre, and a splendid panorama.

Keep following the Great Western Highway to Mount Victoria.

Mount Victoria is classifed as an Urban Conservation Area and has a museum, teashops and a few antiques shops.

Follow the Darling Causeway then turn right onto the Bells Line of Road.

Visit Mount Tomah Botanic Garden, the cool-climate branch of Sydney's Royal Botanic Gardens.

Continue to Windsor, then follow Route 40, and the Western Motorway.

Distance 280km (174 miles)
Time A full day, or stay overnight if possible
Start/end point George Street, central Sydney ✚ *Sydney 3a*
Lunch Café Bon Ton (➤ 102)

HUNTER VALLEY

Wine and wineries are the main attraction of
this large river valley northwest of Sydney,
centred around the town of Cessnock and the village of Pokolbin.
Grapes have been cultivated here since the 1830s and there are
now over 100 wineries in the region; many of these can be toured
and you can, of course, sample the fine wines that originate from
the area. The Hunter also has a reputation for excellent
accommodation and dining, making it a very popular weekend
destination for Sydneysiders.

www.winecountry.com.au

🚆 23K 🚉 Maitland, then a bus to Cessnock

🛈 Hunter Valley Wine Country Visitor Centre ✉ 455 Wine Country Drive,
Pokolbin ☎ (02) 4990 0900 🕐 Mon–Fri 9–5, Sat 9.30–5, Sun 9.30–3.30

KIAMA

One of the closest South Coast resorts to Sydney, the small town
of Kiama (90 minutes' drive away) has long enjoyed great

popularity. As well as good beaches and surfing, the town has a famous blowhole, discovered by whaler George Bass in 1797 on a voyage of coastal exploration, and many historic buildings.

Kiama is close to the charmingly rural Kangaroo Valley, and the Minnamurra Rainforest Centre within the Budderoo National Park.
www.kiama.com.au

➕ 23J 🚂 From Sydney
ℹ️ Kiama Visitor Centre ✉️ Blowhole Point Road ☎️ (02) 4232 3322
🕐 Daily 9–5. Closed 25 Dec

LORD HOWE ISLAND
A true South Sea paradise. Dominated by sheer peaks, this World Heritage-listed small island is just 11km (7 miles) long and 2.8km (1.7 miles) at its widest. The high peaks and lower, scattered hills were created by volcanic activity, and below these lie kentia palm forests, idyllic sandy beaches, a fringing coral reef, and the clear blue waters of the island's lagoon, home to over 500 fish species.
www.lordhoweisland.info

➕ 24K (off map) ✈️ From Sydney and Brisbane
ℹ️ Island Visitor Centre ☎️ 1800 240 937 or (02) 6563 2114 🕐 Mon–Fri 9–4, Sun 9–12.30 ❓ Various grades of accommodation available

MYALL LAKES NATIONAL PARK

This North Coast national park encompasses both a chain of large freshwater lakes and an idyllic 40km (25-mile) coastline. You can rent a houseboat or canoe to explore the lakes, or camp and enjoy surfing and swimming off the golden beaches. The area is particularly appealing to birdwatchers and bushwalkers.

www.nationalparks.nsw.gov.au

 23K ☎ (02) 4984 8200 or (02) 6591 0300 ⊗ Daily 💷 Inexpensive
🅰 No public transport into the park

SNOWY MOUNTAINS

In the state's far south, reached via the town of Jindabyne, this upland region encompasses **Kosciuszko National Park,** where you can ski in winter from the resorts of Thredbo and Perisher Blue. The wilderness park contains heathland and alpine vegetation, as well as Mount Kosciuszko, Australia's highest point (just 2,228m/7,310ft). In summer the area is great for bushwalking, trout fishing, horse riding and mountain biking.

✛ 22J

Kosciuszko National Park

✉ Snowy Region Visitor Centre, Kosciuszko Road, Jindabyne ☎ (02) 6450 5600 🕐 Winter daily 8–5.30; summer daily 8.30–5 🚌 Jindabyne and Thredbo. Perisher Blue (ski season)

SOUTHERN HIGHLANDS

Just 100km (62 miles) from Sydney, this upland region offers a blend of rugged Australian bush, rolling English-type farmland and genteel townships.

Colonial history is well represented: the charming village of Berrima dates from the early 1830s and is full of historic buildings. You can shop for crafts and antiques in Berrima, Moss Vale and Bowral, and go bushwalking in the Morton National Park.

www.southern-highlands.com.au

✚ 23K 🚉 Mittagong, Bowral, Moss Vale, Exeter, Bundanoon

ℹ Information Centre ✉ 62–70 Main Street, Mittagong ☎ 1300 657 559 or (02) 4871 2888 🕐 Daily 8–5.30

HOTELS

NEW SOUTH WALES

SYDNEY

Carlton Crest ($$$)
See page 68.

Hotel Ibis Darling Harbour ($$)
Great views, a popular restaurant and a waterfront location.
✉ 70 Murray Street, Darling Harbour ☎ (02) 9563 0888;
www.ibishotels.com 🚉 Monorail or light rail to Convention

Park Hyatt Sydney ($$$)
One of Sydney's very best hotels, opposite the Opera House.
✉ 7 Hickson Road ☎ (02) 9241 1234; www.sydney.park.hyatt.com
🚌 431–434

Quay Grand Suites ($$$)
See page 68.

The Russell ($$)
Small Victorian hotel with a roof garden, close to the city centre.
✉ 143a George Street, The Rocks ☎ (02) 9241 3543;
www.therussell.com.au 🚉 Circular Quay

BLUE MOUNTAINS

The Mountain Heritage ($$–$$$)
Historic hotel in an ideal location, with superb views and a range of
good-value accommodation.
✉ Corner of Apex and Lovel streets, Katoomba ☎ (02) 4782 2155;
www.mountainheritage.com.au 🚉 Katoomba

COFFS HARBOUR

Break Free Aanuka Beach Resort ($$$)
Set on a sandy beach, this attractive hotel offers suites furnished
with antiques and has delightful gardens.
✉ Firman Drive, Diggers Beach ☎ (02) 6652 7555; www.breakfree.com.au

HUNTER VALLEY
Peppers Convent ($$$)
See page 68.

AUSTRALIAN CAPITAL TERRITORY
CANBERRA
Forrest Inn and Apartments ($–$$)
Good-value rooms and serviced apartments close to Parliament House and the lively Manuka restaurant district.

✉ 30 National Circuit, Forrest ☎ (02) 6295 3433; www.forrestinn.com.au 🚌 39

Hyatt Hotel Canberra ($$$)
The capital's finest hotel, close to the main attractions. A charming 1920s building, with well-maintained gardens in which to relax.

✉ Commonwealth Avenue, Yarralumla ☎ (02) 6270 1234; www.canberra.park.hyatt.com 🚌 31, 39

RESTAURANTS

NEW SOUTH WALES
SYDNEY
Berowra Waters Inn ($$$)
In a beautiful location surrounded by bushland on the Hawksberry River, and serving excellent Modern Australian food.

✉ Near Public Ferry Terminal, Berowa Waters ☎ (02) 9456 1027; www.berowrawatersinn.com 🕐 Lunch Thu–Sun, dinner Thu–Sat 🚌 None, overland access by car ✈ Seaplane from Rosebay

bills ($–$$)
A favourite Sydney spot for relaxed lunching and brunching, with communal newspapers to browse while you sip a cappuccino.

✉ 433 Liverpool Street, Darlinghurst ☎ (02) 9360 9631; www.bills.com.au 🕐 Breakfast and lunch daily, dinner Mon–Sat 🚌 311, 378 or any Oxford Street bus

Doyle's on the Beach ($$$)
See page 61.

Sydney Fish Market ($–$$$)
A wide range of seafood styles and venues.
✉ Bank Street, Pyrmont, Sydney ☎ (02) 9660 1611;
www.sydneyfishmarket.com.au 🚋 Light rail to Fish Market

Tetsuya's ($$$)
French, Japanese and Australian fusion in a high-class setting.
✉ 529 Kent Street ☎ (02) 9267 2900; www.tetsuyas.com 🕐 Dinner
Tue–Sat 🚉 Town Hall

BLUE MOUNTAINS
Café Bon Ton ($–$$)
A lively café in the lovely mountain village of Leura.
✉ 192 The Mall, Leura ☎ (02) 4782 4377; www.bonton.com.au
🕐 Breakfast and lunch daily, dinner Wed–Mon 🚆 Leura

Collits' Inn ($$$)
French cuisine in a historic building on the outskirts of the peaceful
Blue Mountains.
✉ Hartley Vale Road, Hartley Vale ☎ (02) 6355 2072; www.collitsinn.com.au
🕐 Lunch Fri–Sun

BYRON BAY
Fins ($$$)
Byron Bay's finest dining experience. Fresh, gourmet seafood.
✉ Beach Hotel, corner of Jonson and Bay streets ☎ (02) 6685 5029;
www.fins.com.au 🕐 Dinner daily

AUSTRALIAN CAPITAL TERRITORY
CANBERRA
Gus' Cafe ($)
A tiny Canberra institution. Excellent coffee, snacks and mains.
✉ Shop 8, Garema Place, Bunda Street, Canberra City ☎ (02) 6248 8118
🕐 Breakfast, lunch and dinner daily 🚌 Any city centre bus

Juniperberry ($$)
See page 61.

Ottoman Cuisine ($$)
An acclaimed Turkish restaurant specialising in seafood.
✉ Corner Blackall and Broughton Streets, Barton ☎ (02) 6273 6111
🕐 Lunch Tue–Fri, dinner Tue–Sat 🚌 39

SHOPPING

ABORIGINAL ART
Aboriginal and Tribal Art Centre
High-quality paintings, carvings, gifts, jewellery and collectables.
✉ 117 George Street, The Rocks, Sydney ☎ (02) 9247 9625
🚇 Circular Quay

Gavala Aboriginal Cultural Centre
See page 72.

OPALS, GEMS AND JEWELLERY
Flame Opals
One of Sydney's best opal retailers. Offers a good range of stones, both unset and made up into fine jewellery.
✉ 119 George Street, The Rocks, Sydney ☎ (02) 9247 3446
🚇 Circular Quay

Percy Marks Fine Gems
One of Sydney's oldest gem specialists. Opals, Argyle diamonds and South Sea Pearls all set in hand-crafted Australian jewellery.
✉ 60 Elizabeth Street, Sydney ☎ (02) 9233 1355 🚇 Martin Place

DEPARTMENT STORES AND SHOPPING CENTRES
David Jones
One of Australia's very best stores, glamorous 'DJs' operates from two enormous city-centre buildings.
✉ Elizabeth Street and Market Street, Sydney ☎ (02) 9266 5544
🚇 St James

Queen Victoria Building
A vast 1890s building and delightful place to shop. There are over 200 boutiques here.

✉ Corner of George, York and Market streets, Sydney ☎ (02) 9264 9209
🚇 Town Hall

ENTERTAINMENT

NIGHTLIFE

The Entertainment Quarter, Fox Studios

Cinemas, markets (Wed, Sat, Sun), shops, bars and eateries.

✉ Lang Road, Moore Park, Sydney ☎ (02) 9383 4333;
www.entertainmentquarter.com.au 🚌 373, 374, 376, 377, 391–395, 397, 399

Home

A popular nightclub on the waterfront. Bars, dining and dancing.

✉ Cockle Bay Wharf, Darling Harbour, Sydney ☎ (02) 9266 0600;
www.homesydney.com 🕐 Daily 🚝 Monorail to Darling Park

Star City Casino

✉ 80 Pyrmont Street, Pyrmont ☎ (02) 9777 9000; www.starcity.com.au
🕐 24 hours daily 🚝 Light Rail to Star City

THEATRE AND CLASSICAL ENTERTAINMENT

Belvoir St Theatre

An inner-city theatre often showing contemporary Australian plays.

✉ Belvoir Street, Surry Hills, Sydney ☎ (02) 9699 3444; www.belvoir.com.au
🚇 Central

Canberra Theatre Centre

Canberra's main arts venue, for regular opera, ballet and theatre.

✉ Civic Square, London Circuit, Canberra City ☎ (02) 6275 2700;
www.canberratheatre.org.au 🚌 Any city centre bus

Capitol Theatre

A charming old theatre and venue for major musicals.

✉ 13 Campbell Street, Haymarket, Sydney; www.capitoltheatre.com.au
☎ (02) 9320 5000 🚇 Central or Town Hall

Sydney Opera House

See pages 50–51.

Queensland

Occupying an enormous chunk of the continent's northeast, Queensland is the second largest state after Western Australia. From the subtropical capital of Brisbane in the south, this vast tract of land – much of which has a hot, sunny and virtually winterless climate – stretches north to well within the tropics.

Many people come here solely to experience the Great Barrier Reef World Heritage Site, a magnificent natural wonder that lies parallel to the coast's sandy beaches and idyllic islands. But Queensland offers much more. Behind the coastal strip and the hills of the Great Dividing Range, stretches the inhospitable Outback, while in the far north are lush tropical rainforests and the Cape York Peninsula, which ends just south of Papua New Guinea.

www.queenslandholidays.com.au

Brisbane

From its crude beginnings as a penal colony – founded in 1824 as an outpost of New South Wales – and its long-standing reputation as a conservative 'country town', Brisbane has undergone a remarkable metamorphosis in recent years and has embraced progress with much enthusiasm. With a subtropical climate and relatively small population of over 1.6 million, the city has a slower pace of life than that of southern cities, and Queensland's capital has blossomed into a most attractive metropolis.

Although most visitors do not linger for long in Brisbane before heading south to the Gold Coast or north to the attractions of the coast and Great Barrier Reef, there is plenty to see and do here. The city's riverside location is an important ingredient in its charm: Brisbane stands on a sweeping bend of the Brisbane River, and a leisurely cruise or ferry ride along the river is a highlight of any trip.

There *are* museums, galleries and a few graceful old buildings here, but sunny Brisbane is a largely modern city, concerned for the most part with relaxing and enjoying the good things in life. The brilliantly designed South Bank parklands, which include a swimming lagoon and sandy beach, and the city's many parks and gardens, are ideal places to indulge in such pursuits, as are the islands and beaches of nearby Moreton Bay. You can also explore the pleasant city centre – particularly the shops and outdoor cafés of Queen Street Mall; the Riverside Centre and its ferry wharves, just off Eagle Street; and the Roma Street Parkland.

www.ourbrisbane.com

✚ 24L

CITY BOTANIC GARDENS

Brisbane's premier gardens are in a delightful riverside setting and provide the ideal spot for a break from sightseeing and the heat. The gardens are open around the clock. Wander among the palm trees, Bunya pines and rainforest area, or take a guided walk.

✉ Alice Street ☎ (07) 3403 0666 🍴 City Gardens Café (▶ 60) ✋ Free
🚌 The Loop

MOUNT COOT-THA

It's worth making the trip to this peak, 6.5km (4 miles) from the city centre, especially at night, for the wonderful view of Brisbane and its surroundings.

You can visit the **Brisbane Botanic Gardens,** with their tropical and native flora, hiking paths and Aboriginal trails, as well as the Cosmic Skydome and Planetarium, where a dramatic image of the night sky is projected onto a dome.

www.brisbanelookout.com

Brisbane Botanic Gardens

✉ Mount Coot-tha Road, Toowong
☎ (07) 3403 2535 🕔 Sep–Mar daily 8–5.30; Apr–Aug 8–5 ✋ Gardens: free; Skydome: moderate 🍴 Café ($); restaurant ($$) 🚌 471

QUEENSLAND CULTURAL CENTRE

This modern South Bank complex includes two important museums –

the Queensland Art Gallery, with its fine collection of Australian, Aboriginal, Asian, Pacific and European art; and the Queensland Museum with some particularly good Aboriginal and natural history displays.

Nearby to the south, the large riverside South Bank Parklands is one of Australia's best urban parks, with bars, pubs, restaurants and cafés, shopping, an IMAX theatre and weekend markets. The **Queensland Maritime Museum** is also worth a visit.

www.south-bank.net.au

✉ Corner of Melbourne and Grey streets, South Brisbane ☎ Art Gallery: (07) 3840 7303; www.qag.qld.go.au. Museum: (07) 3840 7555; www.qm.qld.gov.au
🕐 Art Gallery: Mon–Fri 10–5, Sat–Sun 9–5. Museum 9.30–5 💰 Free

Queensland Maritime Museum
✉ Stanley Street ☎ (07) 3844 5361 🕐 Daily 9.30–4.30

QUEENSLAND SCIENCENTRE

With over 170 hands-on exhibits, this is the state's largest science and technology centre. Even the most non-scientific mind, young or old, will be captivated and special shows and demonstrations are held daily.

✉ Queensland Museum, corner of Melbourne and Grey streets, South Brisbane ☎ (07) 3840 7555 🕐 Daily 9–5
💰 Moderate

What to See in Queensland

CARNARVON GORGE NATIONAL PARK

Although it is very remote (over 250km/155 miles from the nearest town, Roma), a visit to this spectacular park is well rewarded. The Carnarvon Creek has cut through soft sandstone to create 200m (655ft) cliffs and a 30km (18-mile) long gorge. There is some good bushwalking, as well as lush vegetation and ancient Aboriginal paintings. Roads may be impassable between January and April.
www.epa.qld.gov.au

✚ 11B ✉ Carnarvon National Park, via Rolleston ☎ (07) 4984 4505
🕐 Daily ✋ Free ✖ Roma, then a drive

CAIRNS AND DISTRICT

See pages 38–39.

CHARTERS TOWERS

Once the second largest city in Queensland, with its own stock exchange, this historic town, situated 135km (84 miles) west of Townsville, was built on gold over a century ago. Today it is a living museum of grand hotels, banks and other National Trust-classified buildings. The World Theatre, built in 1891 as an international bank, now serves as a focus for arts and entertainment with a fully restored auditorium, cinema, archival centre and art gallery.

The town has a number of significant events each year, including the Australia Day (26 January) Cricket Festival, the Rodeo (Easter) at nearby Mingela and one of Australia's largest country music festivals on the May Day weekend. (See also Townsville ➤ 116.)

www.charterstowers.qld.gov.au

✚ 11C 🚶 or ✖ Townsville

ℹ Visitor Information Centre ✉ 74 Mosman Street ☎ (07) 4752 0314

🕐 Daily 9–5. Closed Good Fri, 25–26 Dec, 1 Jan

FRASER ISLAND

At 121km (75 miles) long, this extraordinary World Heritage Site is the world's largest sand island. Yet with extensive rainforest, over 40 freshwater lakes, long sandy beaches, and strangely coloured sand cliffs this is a surprisingly varied environment. The wildlife – including dingoes and wallabies – is prolific, making the island the perfect destination for nature lovers and birdwatchers. Fraser Island is reached by vehicular ferry and a four-wheel-drive vehicle is necessary, unless taking one of the many tours.

www.queenslandholidays.com.au

➕ 12B 🖐 Free 🚢 From Hervey Bay 🛈 Hervey Bay Tourism ✉ Corner of Urraween and Maryborough Hervey roads, Hervey Bay ☎ 1800 811 728 or (07) 4125 9855 🕐 Daily 9–5. Closed Good Friday and 25 Dec

GOLD COAST
See pages 40–41.

GREAT BARRIER REEF
See pages 42–43.

LAMINGTON NATIONAL PARK

Temperate and subtropical rainforests, wild mountain scenery with waterfalls, gorges, rock pools, caves and abundant wildlife all combine to make this World Heritage-listed national park a must-see destination for nature lovers. There are 160km (100 miles) of hiking paths to explore, as well as plenty of easy trails and a rainforest canopy trail. The most accessible and popular sections of the national park are Green Mountains and Binna Burra.

www.epa.qld.gov.au

✚ 24L 🤚 Free ✖ Gold Coast or Brisbane, then a drive

ℹ Green Mountains ☎ (07) 5544 0634; Binna Burra ☎ (07) 5533 3584

LONGREACH

Longreach in Queensland's Outback was the first home of the national airline Qantas (Queensland and Northern Territory Aerial Services) during the 1920s, and the town has many charming old buildings. The major attraction is the excellent **Australian Stockman's Hall of Fame** and Outback Heritage Centre – a modern complex that pays tribute to the early explorers, pioneers and settlers.

✚ 10B

Australian Stockman's Hall of Fame

✉ Landsborough Highway, Longreach ☎ (07) 4658 2166 🕐 Daily 9–5. Closed 25 Dec 👆 Expensive 🍴 Snack bar ($) ✈ Longreach

SUNSHINE COAST

Stretching for 65km (40 miles) to the north of Brisbane, the Sunshine Coast region has beautiful white beaches, low-key resorts, and some outstanding national parks. The stylish main resort town of **Noosa Heads** offers sandy beaches and cosmopolitan dining, while nearby attractions include cruising the Noosa River, and exploring the dunes and coloured sand cliffs of Cooloola National Park. Inland, you can tour the Blackall Range region, where there are green hills, charming villages and rich farming country.

www.sunshinecoast.org

🚌 12A 🚊 Nambour, then a bus
✈ Maroochydore
ℹ Tourist Information ✉ Hastings Street, Noosa Heads ☎ (07) 5447 4988 🕐 Daily 9–5. Closed 25 Dec

TOWNSVILLE

With a population of about 125,000, this historic harbourside settlement is Australia's largest tropical city. The main points of interest are the excellent Reef HQ aquarium complex, the Museum of Tropical Queensland housing relics from the wreck HMS *Pandora*, and the wildlife-rich Billabong Sanctuary. You can visit nearby Magnetic Island, with its fine beaches and abundant wildlife, and take trips to the Great Barrier Reef.

www.townsvilleonline.com.au

🚩 11C 🚄 or ✈ Townsville

ℹ Visitor Centre ✉ Flinders Mall ☎ (07) 4721 3660

🕐 Mon–Fri 9–5, Sat–Sun 9–1

WHITSUNDAY ISLANDS

Reached via Proserpine and the villages of Airlie Beach and Shute Harbour, these central coast islands form a very popular holiday destination. There are over 70 islands, mostly hilly and forested, with exquisite beaches and incredibly clear turquoise waters. There is a good choice of resorts – from high-class Hayman to the less sophisticated national park Long Island resort. There are plenty of day trips to the reef, and the region is perfect for sailing, snorkelling and water sports.

www.whitsundaytourism.com

🚩 11C ✈ Proserpine

ℹ Whitsunday Information Centre ✉ Bruce Highway, Proserpine 🕐 Mon–Fri 9–5, Sat–Sun 9–3 ☎ (07) 4945 3711

EXPLORING

a drive ⓞfrom Cairns to the Daintree

This extremely scenic drive takes you beyond the holiday city of Cairns via the coastline to charming Port Douglas and the Daintree's World Heritage-listed rainforest.

From central Cairns, take the Captain Cook Highway north out of town.

Stretching for 30km (18 miles), the beautiful Marlin Coast has many sandy beaches and small resort villages like Trinity Beach and Palm Cove. Other attractions along the way include Cairns Tropical Zoo and Hartley's Crocodile Adventures at Palm Cove, and the Rainforest Habitat near Port Douglas.

Continue on the highway, then take the Port Douglas turn-off.

Once a sleepy fishing settlement, charming Port Douglas is now a rather exclusive resort village, with high-quality accommodation, dining and shopping, a picturesque harbour and a perfect, long sandy beach.

Return to the highway and continue to Mossman.

Mossman has a sugar mill and a few other attractions, but this small town is essentially the gateway to the magnificent Daintree rainforest.

Take the Mossman Gorge Road.

118

This lush region, home to many orchid species; the large, flightless cassowary; birdwing butterflies and a rare tree kangaroo, was World Heritage listed in 1988. The most easily accessible part of the Daintree National Park is Mossman Gorge, with a 2.7km (1.6-mile) circuit hiking trail.

After visiting the gorge, return to the main road to Daintree. Take the turn off to the ferry.

Cross the Daintree River on the car ferry and you can take the bitumen road as far as Cape Tribulation (50km/31 miles). There are several places off this road to experience coastal tropical rainforests and white-sand beaches.

Return to Cairns via the same route.

Distance 320km (200 miles) **Time** A full day
Start/end point Central Cairns ✚ 10D
Lunch On the Inlet ($$) ✉ 3 Inlet Street, Port Douglas
☎ (07) 4099 5255

HOTELS

BRISBANE
Holiday Inn Brisbane ($$)
Good value in a convenient city-centre location – large rooms, two restaurants, bars, a sauna and a gym.

✉ Roma Street ☎ (07) 3238 2222; www.brisbane.holiday-inn.com
🚆 Roma Street Station

Hotel Ibis ($$)
See page 68.

Stamford Plaza Brisbane ($$$)
Luxurious waterfront hotel, close to the Botanic Gardens.

✉ Corner of Edward and Margaret streets ☎ (07) 3221 1999; www.stamford.com.au 🚌 The Loop

CAIRNS
Hotel Sofitel Reef Casino Cairns ($$$)
Part of the Cairns casino complex, this hotel provides all the expected luxuries and a few more besides.

✉ 35–41 Wharf Street ☎ (07) 4030 8801; www.reefcasino.com.au 🚌 None

Reef Palms ($–$$$)
See page 68.

GOLD COAST
Paros on the Beach ($$)
Right on the beach, Paros has 35 Mediterranean-style apartments.

✉ 26 Old Burleigh Road, Surfers Paradise ☎ (07) 5592 0780; www.parosonthebeach.com 🚌 1, 1A

SUNSHINE COAST
Netanya Noosa ($$)
This delightful low-rise resort, on the beachfront, offers luxury and relaxation at an affordable price.

✉ 75 Hastings Street, Noosa Heads ☎ (07) 5447 4722; www.netanyanoosa.com.au 🚌 None

RESTAURANTS

BRISBANE
Baguette ($$–$$$)
Renowned restaurant. French, Australian and Asian influences.
✉ 150 Racecourse Road, Ascot ☎ (07) 3268 6168; www.baguette.com.au
🕒 Lunch and dinner 🚌 300, 303

City Gardens Café ($–$$)
See page 60.

Pier Nine ($$)
An excellent riverside seafood restaurant.
✉ Eagle Street Pier, Brisbane ☎ (07) 3226 2100; www.piernine.com.au
🕒 Dinner Mon–Sat 🛳 Riverside

TROPICAL NORTH QUEENSLAND
Nautilus ($$$)
Fine seafood is the speciality of this restaurant, set in a rainforest.
✉ 17 Murphy Street, Port Douglas ☎ (07) 4099 5330;
www.nautilus-restaurant.com.au 🕒 Dinner 🚌 None

SUNSHINE COAST
Ricky Ricardos ($$–$$$)
Comfortable restaurant with modern dishes in a riverside setting.
✉ Noosa Wharf, Quamby Place, Noosa Heads ☎ (07) 5447 2455 🕒 Lunch
and dinner 🚌 None

The Spirit House ($$)
Although it's located inland from the coast, this superb Asian-style
restaurant, in a unique rainforest setting, is well worth a visit.
✉ 20 Ninderry Road, Yandina ☎ (07) 5446 8994; www.spirithouse.com.au
🕒 Lunch daily, dinner Wed–Sat 🚌 None

SHOPPING

AUSTRALIANA
Australian Woolshed
This major attraction has an excellent gift shop (► 70).

ABORIGINAL ART
Queensland Aboriginal Creations
See page 72.

OPALS, GEMS AND JEWELLERY
Quilpie Opals
Leading opal specialist selling stones direct from the mines.
✉ Lennons Plaza, 68 Queen Street, Brisbane ☎ (07) 3221 7369 🚌 The Loop

SHOPPING CENTRES
Marina Mirage
A waterfront Gold Coast shopping centre with 80 speciality shops, boutiques and art galleries.
✉ Seaworld Drive, Broadwater Spit, Main Beach, Gold Coast
☎ (07) 5577 0088 🚌 1, 1A

ENTERTAINMENT

NIGHTLIFE
The Arena
This buzzing venue features live bands, DJs and dancing.
✉ 210 Brunswick Street, Fortitude Valley, Brisbane ☎ (07) 3252 5690
🕐 Daily 🚌 121, 204, 300

Conrad Jupiters Casino
The brash Gold Coast is the perfect venue for this glitzy casino.
✉ Gold Coast Highway, Broadbeach, Gold Coast ☎ (07) 5592 8100;
www.conrad.com.au 🕐 Daily 🚌 1,1A

Friday's Riverside
Large nightclub with water views, restaurants, bars and live bands.
✉ Riverside Centre, 123 Eagle Street, Brisbane ☎ (07) 3832 2122;
www.fridays.com.au 🕐 Daily 🚌 The Loop

Press Club
The city's trendiest café and bar, with live music and DJs.
✉ Corner of Brunswick and Ann streets, Fortitude Valley, Brisbane
☎ (07) 3852 4000 🕐 Tue–Sun 🚌 121, 204, 300

Victoria and Tasmania

**Australia's most southerly states hold many surprises –
a cooler climate (including winter snows) than many
would expect, tranquil farmland,
rugged peaks, and coastlines
lashed by the wild waters of Bass
Strait, which divides Victoria from
Tasmania.**

Victoria, separated from New South Wales by
the country's longest river, the Murray, is small
and densely populated by Australian standards.
From the gracious capital, Melbourne, it is easy to reach
attractions that vary from dramatic coastlines to the ski fields and
peaks of the Great Dividing Range.

The compact island state of Tasmania is packed with interest.
Its violent convict past intrigues history lovers, while the superb
coastal, mountain and wilderness scenery provides endless
opportunities for outdoor activities. You can fly to Hobart and
Launceston from the mainland, or take the *Spirit of Tasmania* ferry
from Melbourne or Sydney to Devonport.

www.visitvictoria.com
www.discovertasmania.com.au

Melbourne

Australia's second largest city, with a population of around 3.5 million, Melbourne is very different to its glossy northern sister. Founded long after Sydney, in 1835, this more elegant, European-style city retains many grand buildings and while its citizens are regarded as more conservative than Sydneysiders, this is not borne out in any tangible way. The climate is often 'four seasons in a day' and can be very hot in summer. Melbourne's cooler winter temperatures are often accompanied by romantic, grey days.

Melbourne has much to recommend it to visitors: there are over 4,000 restaurants and the dining scene is superb; the shopping rivals that of Sydney; sport is practically a religion; and there is plenty of nightlife – including high-quality theatrical and cultural events at the Victorian Arts Centre and other venues.

A vibrant and dynamic city, bisected by the Yarra River (on which you can take a scenic cruise), the central city area contains many museums and galleries, gracious avenues such as Collins and Spring Streets, and an abundance of green open spaces. Another Melbourne delight is riding the extensive tram network; trams have practically disappeared from all other Australian cities, but in Melbourne this is very much the way to get around.

This is a city of many ethnic groups, as a visit to Chinatown and the Museum of Chinese Australian History, or the suburbs of Italian-influenced Carlton and multicultural Richmond reveal. Other enclaves are St Kilda (▶ 128–129) and South Yarra, with boutiques and the grand 1840s house, Como.

www.visitmelbourne.com

✚ 21J

MELBOURNE CRICKET GROUND

Visiting this most hallowed of Australia's sporting venues is a must. The city's famous cricket ground, known as the MCG, was the site of the first Australia-England test match in 1877 and the main stadium for the 1956 Olympic Games. Today, the 100,000-capacity ground is used for both cricket and Australian Rules

Football, and contains the excellent Olympic and Australian Cricket Hall of Fame.

www.mcg.org.au

✉ Yarra Park, Jolimont ☎ (03) 9657 8864 🕒 Daily 9.30–4.30. Closed Good Fri, 25 Dec 🖐 Moderate 🍴 Coffee shop ($) 🚊 Trams 48, 75 ❓ Regular guided tours 10–3 on non-event days

MELBOURNE MUSEUM

This modern complex is the largest museum in the southern hemisphere. Highlights include the Science and Life Gallery, the Bunjilaka Aboriginal Centre, a 'living forest'

complete with wildlife, and an IMAX theatre.

www.melbourne.museum.vic.gov.au

✉ Carlton Gardens, Rathdowne Street ☎ 13 1102 🖐 Moderate 🚊 Trams 86, 96, City Circle

MELBOURNE OBSERVATION DECK

The view from this observation deck, on Level 55 of the tallest building in Melbourne, is simply awe-inspiring. The panorama takes in the city and Port Phillip Bay and stretches as far away as the Dandenong Ranges, about 40km (25 miles) from Melbourne.

www.melbournedeck.com.au

✉ 525 Collins Street ☎ (03) 9629 8222 🕐 Daily 10–9 💷 Moderate
🍴 Licensed café ($$) 🚋 City Circle tram

NATIONAL GALLERY OF VICTORIA

Victoria's premier art gallery displays some of the finest artwork in Australia. The international collection, featuring European Old Masters, photography and Asian, pre-Columbian and contemporary art, is housed at the revamped **NGV International**

on St Kilda Road. The Ian
Potter Centre: NGV Australia,
at Federation Square, contains
Australian art, including
Aboriginal, Colonial and
contemporary works.
www.ngv.vic.gov.au
NGV International
✉ 180 St Kilda Road ☎ (03) 8620
2222 🕐 Daily 10–5. Closed Good
Fri, 25 Dec ✋ Free general
admission 🚌 City Circle tram,
6, 8, 72

OLD MELBOURNE GAOL

Although rather grim, this mid-19th century building is fascinating. The gaol, scene of 135 hangings – including that of the notorious bushranger Ned Kelly on 11 November 1880 – provides an idea of what colonial 19th-century prison life was like, and contains many intriguing exhibits, including death masks and a flogging triangle. ✉ Russell Street ☎ (03) 9663 7228 🕐 Daily 9.30–5. Closed Good Fri, 25 Dec and Anzac Day am 🖐 Moderate 🚌 City Circle tram ❓ Atmospheric evening tours available

ST KILDA

Melbourne has many lively suburbs which provide a venue for Melburnians to let their hair down. Located on the shores of Port

Phillip Bay, St Kilda has been the city's seaside resort since the 1880s, when the pier was constructed. Its waterfront pathway is popular with walkers, cyclists and in-line skaters, and the Luna Park funfair, built in 1912, continues to be a great attraction. There are dozens of bustling cafés and restaurants, particularly on Acland Street. The Sunday arts and crafts markets are good, and you can take a cruise on the bay from the St Kilda Pier.

www.visitvictoria.com

🚃 Any St Kilda tram

ℹ️ Melbourne Visitor Information Centre ✉️ Federation Square ☎ (03) 9658 9658 🕐 Daily 9–6

a walk around the Yarra River, Kings Domain and Botanic Gardens

This walk ventures beyond Melbourne's city centre, along the Yarra River and into the large area of parkland to the south.

Start at Flinders Street Station (corner of Swanston and Flinders Streets), then cross Princes Bridge and turn right for Southbank Promenade.

There are many temptations here in the large Southgate shopping and eating complex. If you can, just admire the view of the city and river from the promenade and continue walking.

Walk under Princes Bridge and follow the path beside the river.

After walking along the Yarra, head away from the water at Swan Street Bridge and into the Kings Domain. This lush parkland encompasses impressive Government House, the official residence of the Governor of Victoria.

Continue into the gardens.

The delightful Royal Botanic Gardens are centred around an extensive ornamental lake. They contain some 60,000 plant species and are one of central Melbourne's most attractive features.

Follow the signs to La Trobe's Cottage.

The Cottage, a modest mid-19th-century dwelling, was the home of Charles La Trobe, Victoria's first governor from 1851 to 1854. It stands in contrast to the large Shrine of Remembrance near by, which contains an important war memorial.

From here you can either cross St Kilda Road and take a tram to Flinders Street Station, or walk back via the Kings Domain and stop in at the National Gallery (▶ 126–127).

Distance 4 km (2.5 miles)
Time 2–4 hours, including time for a light lunch
Start/end point Flinders Street Station
🚋 City Circle tram
Lunch Observatory Cafe ($–$$) ✉ Royal Botanic Gardens ☎ (03) 9650 5600

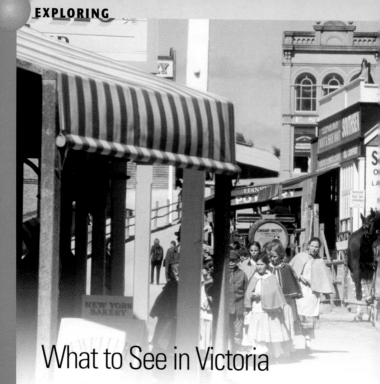

What to See in Victoria

BALLARAT

Gold was discovered near Ballarat in 1851, an event that was to bring incredible wealth to the colony, and this elegant city still contains many grand buildings from those days. The main attraction is the excellent **Sovereign Hill** historical park, a re-creation of the gold rush era. Other sights are the Ballarat Wildlife Park and Ballarat Fine Art Gallery.

www.visitballarat.com.au

✛ 21J

Sovereign Hill

✉ Bradshaw Street ☎ (03) 5337 1100 ⏰ Daily 10–5. Closed 25 Dec 💲 Expensive

DANDENONG RANGES

Just 40km (25 miles) east of Melbourne are the delightful Dandenong Ranges – cool, moist hills cloaked with eucalypts and rainforest. Their many attractions include Puffing Billy, a quaint steam train which runs between Belgrave and Gembrook, and the William Ricketts Sanctuary, an unusual park featuring Aboriginal-themed sculptures.

www.parkweb.vic.gov.au
www.yarrarangestourism.com
✚ 21J 🚉 Upper Ferntree Gully or Belgrave
ℹ Visitor Centre ✉ 1211 Burwood Highway, Upper Ferntree Gully ☎ 1800 645 505 or (03) 9758 7522 🕔 Daily 9–5. Closed Good Fri, 25 Dec

GREAT OCEAN ROAD

See pages 44–45.

PHILLIP ISLAND

This scenic island, linked by bridge to the mainland, is famous for its nightly Penguin Parade – tiny fairy penguins waddling ashore to their burrows. The site of the parade and its visitor centre at

Summerland Beach are part of the **Phillip Island Nature Park,** which incorporates the island's Koala Conservation Centre (near the main town of Cowes), the ideal place to meet these cuddly marsupials.

www.visitphillipisland.com
www.penguins.org.au
 21H

⋯ Visitor Information Centre
✉ 895 Phillip Island Tourist Road,
Newhaven ☎ 1300 366 422 or
(03) 5956 7447 🕓 Daily 9–5
Phillip Island Nature Park
☎ (03) 5951 2800 🕓 Koala Centre:
daily 10–5.30. Penguin Centre: daily
from 10am 👋 Moderate 🚌 From
Melbourne

WILSONS PROMONTORY NATIONAL PARK

The spectacular 'Prom' forms the Australian mainland's most southerly point. This is one of Victoria's most popular national parks, offering beaches and superb coastal scenery, rainforests, well-marked hiking trails, and a wide range of flora and fauna.

www.parkweb.vic.gov.au
✚ 22H 👋 Inexpensive
⋯ Visitor Centre ✉ Tidal River
☎ (03) 5680 9555 🕓 Daily from
8.30am

Hobart

Tasmania's capital is one of Australia's most pleasant settlements. The small city of Hobart, on the River Derwent, is full of old colonial buildings; walking is the best way to appreciate the historic atmosphere. While here, take a river cruise and a trip to Mount Wellington (1,270m/4,167ft), which dominates the city – the view is sensational.
www.discovertasmania.com.au
 22G

BATTERY POINT

With its charming mid-19th-century cottages and houses, craft and antiques shops and quaint

streets like Arthur's Circus, this inner city 'village' is Hobart's showpiece. Highlights are the **Narryna Heritage Museum** and the 1818 Signal Station and military base from which the suburb takes its name.

Narryna Heritage Museum

✉ 103 Hampden Road ☎ (03) 6234 2791 🕐 Mon–Fri 10.30–5, Sat–Sun 2–5. Closed Good Fri, Anzac Day, 25 Dec ✋ Inexpensive

ROYAL TASMANIAN BOTANICAL GARDENS

These gardens, set high overlooking the river and full of native and exotic plants, form part of the large area of parkland known as the Queens Domain. They include a Conservatory, a Tropical Glasshouse and a museum of botany and horticulture.

www.rtbg.tas.gov.au

✉ Queens Domain ☎ (03) 6236 3075 ⊕ Daily from 8am 🖐 Free general admission 🍴 Restaurant ($$)

SALAMANCA PLACE

This delightful old dockside street is lined with sandstone warehouses converted into restaurants and arts and crafts shops, and is the venue for Hobart's lively Saturday market (► 77). Antarctic Adventure, in neighbouring Salamanca Square, is well worth a visit, and nearby Sullivans Cove is where the first settlers landed in 1804.

www.salamanca.com.au

✉ Salamanca Place ⏰ Markets: Sat 8.30–3 ⌨ Free 🍴 Many cafés and restaurants ($–$$$)

TASMANIAN MUSEUM AND ART GALLERY

Hobart's Tasmanian Museum contains some fine and varied exhibits, particularly on Australian mammals, convict history and the Indigenous Tasmanians. The attached art gallery holds a good collection of colonial art. An ideal place to discover the island's history.

www.tmag.tas.gov.au

✉ 40 Macquarie Street ☎ (03) 6211 4177 ⏰ Daily 10–5. Closed Good Fri, 25 Dec and Anzac Day ⌨ Free

What to See in Tasmania

FREYCINET PENINSULA

Tasmania's east coast is renowned for beautiful scenery, none of which surpasses that of **Freycinet National Park** with its sandy white beaches, granite peaks and abundance of flora, birds and animals. The park is reached via the fishing settlement of Coles Bay. The town of Bicheno has more lovely beaches, great diving, a Sealife Centre and wildlife park.

www.dpiwe.tas.gov.au

✛ 22G 🚌 Tassie Link to Bicheno or Coles Bay 🛈 Visitor Centre
✉ Freycinet Drive, Freycinet NP ☎ (03) 6256 7000 ⏰ Daily 8–6; winter 8–5

LAUNCESTON

Tasmania's second city, situated on the Tamar River and founded in 1805 (a year after Hobart), has retained many of its old buildings, which can be viewed on a self-guided walk around town. There are pleasant parks and reserves – a visit to the spectacular Cataract Gorge Reserve is recommended. The Queen Victoria Museum and Art Gallery, located at two sites (city centre and across the river at Inveresk) is also worth a visit. The Launceston region is rich in historic houses and wineries.

www.discovertasmania.com.au

➕ 22H 🚌 or ✈ Launceston

ℹ Information Centre ✉ 12–16 St John Street ☎ (03) 6336 3133

🕐 Mon–Fri 9–5, Sat 9–3, Sun 9–12

THE MIDLANDS

The Midlands Highway, running for 200km (124 miles) between Hobart and Launceston, passes through charming and historic towns. Oatlands is full of atmospheric old buildings such as the Court House, while, further north, picturesque Ross is famous for its 1836 bridge and contains the **Tasmanian Wool Centre**, devoted to the state's extensive wool industry.

➕ 22G

Tasmanian Wool Centre

✉ Church Street, Ross ☎ (03) 6381 5466 🕐 Daily 9–5 ✋ Inexpensive

🚌 Tasmanian Redline from Hobart

PORT ARTHUR AND THE TASMAN PENINSULA

Established as a far-flung penal settlement for the worst convict offenders in 1830, Port Arthur has over 30 ruins and historic sites, an excellent museum, and the settlement's poignant burial ground, the Isle of the Dead.

The surrounding Tasman Peninsula has magnificent scenery on the east coast, the Tasmanian Devil Park with an excellent wildlife collection, and the scenic Bush Mill Steam Railway.

www.portarthur.org.au

🚌 22G ✉ Port Arthur Historic Site
☎ 1800 659 101 or (03) 6251 2300
🕐 Daily 8.30–dusk ✋ Expensive;
includes cruise and guided walk
🚌 Tassie Link from Hobart

STRAHAN

The lightly populated west coast is a region of wild coastline, rivers and forest lands. From the waterside village of Strahan (pronounced 'Strawn') you can go fishing, take a scenic flight, and cruise Macquarie Harbour – once the site of the brutal Sarah Island penal settlement – and the pristine Gordon River, part of the World Heritage-listed Franklin-Gordon Wild Rivers National Park. In town, the **Strahan Visitor Centre** provides a fascinating lesson in local history.

🚌 21G

Strahan Visitor Centre

✉ The Esplanade ☎ (03) 6471 7622 🕐 Daily 10–6 ✋ Inexpensive
🚌 Tassie Link to Strahan

TASMANIA'S WORLD HERITAGE AREA

See pages 52–53.

HOTELS

VICTORIA
MELBOURNE
Novotel St Kilda ($$)
A large hotel on Port Phillip Bay with a spa, heated pool and gym.
✉ 16 The Esplanade, St Kilda, Melbourne ☎ (03) 9525 5522;
www.novotelstkilda.com.au 🚋 Any St Kilda tram

The Victoria Hotel ($–$$)
See page 69.

Sheraton Towers Southgate ($$$)
See page 69.

TASMANIA
HOBART
Corus Hotel Hobart ($$)
Centrally located, good-value hotel, with pleasant rooms.
✉ 156 Bathurst Street, Hobart, Tasmania ☎ (03) 6232 6255;
www.corushotels.com.au 🚋 None

Somerset on the Pier ($$$)
See page 69.

RESTAURANTS

VICTORIA
MELBOURNE
Donovan's ($$–$$$)
Right on the St Kilda's seafront, serving superb Italian fare.
✉ 40 Jacka Boulevard, St Kilda ☎ (03) 9534 8221 🕐 Lunch and dinner
daily 🚋 Any St Kilda tram.

Flower Drum ($$$)
High-quality Chinese restaurant with a delicious, unusual menu.
✉ 17 Market Lane ☎ (03) 9662 3655 🕐 Lunch Mon–Sat, dinner daily
🚋 City Circle tram

Jimmy Watson's Wine Bar and Restaurant ($$)
Popular wine bar with great meals, able to accommodate groups.
✉ 333 Lygon Street, Carlton ☎ (03) 9347 5205; www.jimmywatsons.com.au

Nudel Bar ($)
See page 61.

BALLARAT
The Ansonia ($$)
Excellent Modern Australian cuisine in a smart boutique hotel.
✉ 32 Lydiard Street South ☎ (03) 5332 4678 🕐 Breakfast, lunch and dinner

GREAT OCEAN ROAD
Chris's Beacon Point Restaurant ($$–$$$)
Inventive seafood and Greek-influenced meals and an ocean view.
✉ 280 Skennes Creek Road, near Apollo Bay ☎ (03) 5237 6411 🕐 Lunch and dinner daily

The Victoria Hotel ($$)
A beautifully renovated pub serving Modern Australian cuisine.
✉ 42 Bank Street, Port Fairy ☎ (03) 5568 2891 🕐 Lunch and dinner daily

PHILLIP ISLAND
The Jetty ($$)
The island's premier restaurant. Fresh local lobster and seafood.
✉ The Esplanade, Cowes ☎ (03) 5952 2060 🕐 Lunch Sat–Sun, dinner daily

TASMANIA
HOBART
Annapurna ($–$$)
Inexpensive, excellent Indian food and good vegetarian options.
✉ 305 Elizabeth Street, North Hobart ☎ (03) 6236 9500;
www.annapurnaindiancuisine.com 🕐 Lunch Mon–Fri, dinner daily

Lebrina ($$–$$$)
Wonderful European cuisine just north of the city centre.
✉ 155 New Town Road, New Town ☎ (03) 6228 7775 🕐 Dinner Tue–Sat

Maldini ($$)
Popular café with great coffee and a range of good Italian meals.
✉ 47 Salamanca Place ☎ (03) 6223 4460 🕐 Breakfast, lunch and dinner

Mures Upper Deck ($$–$$$)
See page 61.

DEVONPORT
The Deck Café & Restaurant ($$)
An excellent range of local seafood, overlooking the Mersey River.
✉ 188–190 Tarleton Street East ☎ (03) 6427 7188;
www.thedeckcafe.com.au 🕐 Brunch, lunch and dinner Mon–Sat, brunch Sun

LAUNCESTON
Fee and Me ($$–$$$)
One of Tasmania's best Modern Australian restaurants.
✉ 190 Charles Street ☎ (03) 6331 3195; www.feeandme.com.au 🕐 Dinner
Mon–Sat

Star Bar Café ($–$$)
Grab a snack, coffee and cake, or a good-value meal.
✉ 113 Charles Street ☎ (03) 6331 6111 🕐 Lunch and dinner daily

PORT ARTHUR
Felons Restaurant ($$)
Creates innovative dishes from the best local produce.
✉ Visitor Centre, Port Arthur Historic Site ☎ (03) 6251 2310 🕐 Dinner daily

SHOPPING

AUSTRALIANA
Body Map
See page 73.

Chapel Street
A lively shopping street stretching through South Yarra and Prahan
in the inner-city.
✉ South Yarra and Prahran, Melbourne 🚋 Trams 6, 8, 72

Naturally Tasmanian
See page 73.

ABORIGINAL ARTS
Aboriginal Art Galleries of Australia
See page 72.

Tiagarra Aboriginal Cultural Centre and Museum
Aboriginal centre and museum, also selling quality arts and crafts.
✉ Mersey Bluff, Bluff Road, Devonport, Tasmania ☎ (03) 6424 8250

CRAFTS
Convent Gallery
Restored former nunnery, with fine art, jewellery, food and wine.
✉ Cnr Hill and Daly Streets, Daylesford, Victoria ☎ (03) 5348 3211 🚌 None

Potoroo
Melbourne outlet with artworks, unusual ceramics and glassware.
✉ Southgate Arts and Leisure Precinct, Melbourne ☎ (03) 9690 9859
🚌 City Circle tram

Saddlers Court Gallery
A collection of shops in a historic village 30 minutes from Hobart.
✉ 48–50 Bridge Street, Richmond, Tasmania ☎ (03) 6260 2132
🚌 Tasmanian Redline from Hobart

ENTERTAINMENT
The Arts Centre
✉ 100 St Kilda Road, Melbourne ☎ (03) 9281 8000 🚌 Tram 3, 5, 6, 8

Princess Theatre
✉ 163 Spring Street, Melbourne ☎ (03) 9299 9800 🚌 City Circle tram

Theatre Royal
✉ 29 Campbell Street, Hobart ☎ (03) 6233 2299 🚌 None

South Australia and the Northern Territory

Founded in 1836 and settled by non-convicts, South Australia has an extraordinary range of scenery. There are fertile farming and wine-producing regions outside Adeliade in the south, but the majority of the land is taken up by the arid deserts and peaks of the Outback.

Originally part of South Australia, the sparsely populated Northern Territory is still real frontier country. Almost half of the population, a large proportion of which are Aboriginal people, lives in cosmopolitan Darwin. From the tropical 'Top End' to the desert lands of the 'Red Centre' around Alice Springs, the Northern Territory is endlessly fascinating, with superb natural attractions like Kakadu and Uluṟu.

The 2,979km (1,861 miles) between Adelaide and Darwin is now connected by the famous Ghan train, which takes two nights to cover the distance.

www.southaustralia.com
www.travelnt.com

Adelaide

South Australia's capital was first settled in December 1836, when HMS *Buffalo* docked at Glenelg with her 'cargo' of free settlers. Unlike many Australian cities, Adelaide was planned – Englishman Colonel William Light was responsible for the grid of city-centre streets. Adelaide was once known as the 'City of Churches' and for its conservative citizens, but today the 1.1 million population enjoys an enviable lifestyle and a Mediterranean climate.

Surrounded by large areas of parkland, and with the Adelaide Hills forming a splendid backdrop, Adelaide's compact and mostly flat city centre is a delightful place to explore; there are many old buildings, relatively little traffic, and a sense of calm which is rare in urban environments. This elegant city is famous for its café and restaurant scene, as well as for a thriving artistic and cultural life. The ideal time to be here is during the biennial (every even-numbered year), internationally acclaimed Adelaide Festival of Arts, when the city comes alive with everything from classical music concerts to outrageous fringe theatre.

In addition to visiting the museums and attractions detailed below, you should take a cruise on the placid and scenic River Torrens, which passes through the city. Within the metropolitan area, you can also visit the charming seaside suburb of Glenelg, where the first settlers landed in 1836 – it can be reached by an enjoyable tram ride from the city centre. The historic settlement of Port Adelaide was once the city's harbour town, but now concentrates on its heritage attractions, including the South Australian Maritime Museum and the National Railway Museum complex, the largest of its kind in the country.

www.adelaide.southaustralia.com

 19J

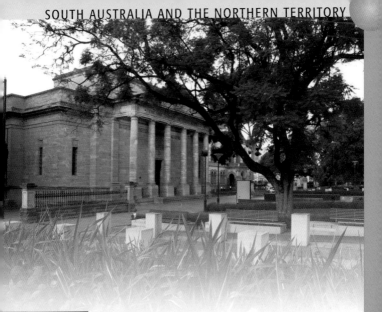

ART GALLERY OF SOUTH AUSTRALIA AND NORTH TERRACE

A stroll down North Terrace, Adelaide's grandest avenue, is the best way to see the city's historic buildings, several of which are open to the public. At the western end are the Adelaide Casino in a restored 1920s railway station, Old Parliament House, and the latter's neighbouring, much more impressive successor. East of King William Street lie the South Australian Museum, the Art Gallery of South Australia, and 1840s Ayers House, former home of Sir Henry Ayers, who was seven times Premier of South Australia and the inspiration behind the naming of Ayers Rock.

www.artgallery.sa.gov.au

✉ Art Gallery of South Australia: North Terrace ☎ (08) 8207 7000 🕐 Daily 10–5. Closed Good Fri am, 25 Dec 🖐 Free general admission 🍴 Art Gallery Café ($–$$) 🚌 City Loop ❓ Free guided tours at regular intervals

GLENELG

Take the vintage tram from Victoria Square in the city to this popular seaside suburb where you can soak up the history and have a relaxed lunch in one of the many excellent eating establishments. Walk the pier and be sure to check out the replica of the HMS *Buffalo*, where there is an interesting museum and a popular family restaurant.

✉ Glenelg Visitor Centre, Foreshore ☎ (08) 8294 5833 🕐 Mon–Fri 9–5, Sat–Sun 10–3 ✋ Free 🚌 Glenelg tram or 138 bus

SOUTH AUSTRALIAN MUSEUM

In addition to the usual natural history and general ethnographic and anthropological displays, this better-than-average museum has an internationally acclaimed collection of Aboriginal Australian artefacts. Another highlight is the large Pacific Cultures exhibit.

www.samuseum.sa.gov.au

✉ North Terrace ☎ (08) 8207 7500 🕐 Daily 10–5. Closed Good Fri, 25 Dec ✋ Free 🚌 City Loop

TANDANYA NATIONAL ABORIGINAL CULTURAL INSTITUTE

This illuminating Aboriginal centre is one of a few of its kind in Australia. Including galleries with high-quality changing art exhibitions, workshops, and an area for dance and other performing arts, Tandanya (the local Aboriginal name for the Adelaide region) is a must for visitors. The centre has a shop selling gifts and a variety of good Aboriginal-made items.

www.tandanya.com.au

✉ 253 Grenfell Street ☎ (08) 8224 3200 🕐 Daily 10–5 ✋ Inexpensive 🚌 City Loop

a walk around North Adelaide and the City Parklands

An easy walk which takes you beyond the city centre and into some of Adelaide's delightful parklands.

Start on King William Road, just beyond the junction with North Terrace.

The Adelaide Festival Centre is the heart of Adelaide's arts scene. The large modern building houses several performance halls and a performing arts museum. River cruises start in front of the centre.

Continue north on King William Road, crossing the River Torrens on Adelaide Bridge.

St Peter's Cathedral dates from 1869; the bells are the heaviest and finest in the southern hemisphere.

Walk along Pennington Terrace to reach Montefiore Hill.

From the lookout, 'Light's Vision', next to the statue of Colonel William Light, there are wonderful views.

Walk up Jeffcott Street towards Wellington Square, then turn right at Archer Street to reach O'Connell Street.

The elegant suburb of North Adelaide contains many grand old homes. A lively pub, café and gallery scene thrives along O'Connell and Melbourne streets.

From O'Connell Street, turn left into Brougham Place, then right into Frome Road to reach Melbourne Street. Return to Frome Road and cross the River Torrens via Albert Bridge to Adelaide's small zoo.

Australia's oldest zoo, it has aviaries, a reptile house and an entertaining collection of Australian mammals.

Follow the signs to the Botanic Garden.

Don't miss the garden's Bicentennial Conservatory, a vast, glass dome containing a tropical rainforest; or the nearby National Wine Centre.

Return to North Terrace.

Distance 4km (2.5 miles)
Time 2–4 hours, depending on time at the zoo and in the gardens
Start point Adelaide Festival Centre 🚌 City Loop
End point North Terrace 🚌 City Loop
Lunch The Oxford Hotel (▶ 169)

What to See in South Australia

ADELAIDE HILLS

Just 20 minutes east of the city, this region of hills, bushland, vineyards and picturesque small towns is a popular weekend destination. Attractions include good views from the summit of Mount Lofty, botanic gardens, the acclaimed National Motor Museum at Birdwood, and Warrawong Earth Sanctuary – an important wildlife reserve. The German-style main town of Hahndorf has fine artworks in the Hahndorf Academy.

www.visitadelaidehills.com.au

✚ 19J 🚌 From Adelaide

ℹ Visitor Information Centre ✉ 41 Main Street, Hahndorf ☎ (08) 8388 1185

🕐 Mon–Fri 9–5, Sat–Sun 10–4

BAROSSA VALLEY

The wine-producing area of the Barossa was settled in the 1830s by Silesians and Prussians, and this picturesque valley is characterised by distinctive European architecture, traditions and cuisine. You can visit some of the 50 or so wineries, and enjoy the ambience of towns and villages like Tanunda, Bethany, Lyndoch and Angaston.

www.barossa-region.org

✚ 19J 🚌 or 🚂 From Adelaide

ℹ Barossa Wine and Visitor Information Centre ✉ 66–68 Murray Street, Tanunda ☎ 1300 852 982 or (08) 8563 0600 🕐 Mon–Fri 9–5, Sat–Sun 10–4. Closed Good Fri, 25 Dec

FLINDERS RANGES NATIONAL PARK

A rugged desert mountain chain containing one of the most ancient landscapes on earth. Plenty of wildlife can be found, while there are several good hikes that allow you to see the diverse plantlife. The highlights of the Park are Wilpena Pound, an enormous 80sq km (30 sq miles) elevated amphitheatre surrounded by sheer cliffs, and St Mary's Peak (1,165m/3,822ft), a challenging walk for experienced hikers. The area is rich in Aboriginal art.

www.environment.sa.gov.au

🚻 19K 👣 Inexpensive 🚌 or ✖ From Adelaide
ℹ Wilpena Pound Visitor Centre ☎ (08) 8648 0048 🕐 Daily 8–6

KANGAROO ISLAND

Australia's third largest island is a relaxed place with spectacular scenery, remarkable wildlife, and pleasant small towns like the main settlement of Kingscote. There are rugged cliffs and sandy beaches; a large part of the island is within Flinders Chase National Park, domain of kangaroos, koalas and prolific birdlife; and you can view Australian sea lions from close quarters at Seal Bay Conservation Park.

www.tourkangarooisland.com.au

🞢 19J 🞨 From Adelaide 🚢 From Cape Jervis

ℹ️ Kangaroo Island Gateway Visitor Centre ✉️ Howard Drive, Pennesaw ☎️ 1800 811 080 or (08) 8553 1185 🕐 Mon–Fri 9–5, Sat–Sun 10–4. Closed 25 Dec

Darwin

The Northern Territory's capital and largest city was founded in 1869. Situated closer to Asia than to any major Australian cities, it has a multicultural population of about 108,000. Darwin was bombed by the Japanese during World War II, and suffered another catastrophe in 1974, when Cyclone Tracy virtually flattened the city. Located on vast Darwin Harbour (on which a cruise is highly recommended), this tropical, modern settlement is a laid-back place. Few reminders of Darwin's history remain, but you can visit the 1883 Fannie Bay Gaol and take a historical walk around the city centre.

www.travelnt.com ✚ 6E

DARWIN WHARF PRECINCT

This busy waterfront complex includes shops, cafés and restaurants, and you can go fishing or take a boat excursion from the wharf. The Australian Pearling Exhibition is here, as are the Indo Pacific Marine – an award-winning education and environment centre – and the Deckchair Outdoor Cinema.

📧 Stokes Hill Wharf ☎ (08) 8981 4268 ⏰ Precinct: daily. Attractions: 10–5 ✋ Attractions: moderate

GEORGE BROWN DARWIN BOTANIC GARDENS

Containing the southern hemisphere's most extensive collection of tropical palms, an orchid farm, a rainforest area and wetlands flora, Darwin's gardens are a delightful place in which to relax or escape the heat.

✉ Geranium Street, The Gardens ☎ (08) 8981 1958 🕐 Daily 7–7 ✋ Free

MINDIL BEACH

Although swimming is not recommended due to box jellyfish, sharks and crocodiles, this pleasant beach offers a park, wonderful sunsets, Darwin's casino and the famous **Mindil Beach Sunset Markets** (▶ 77).

Mindil Beach Sunset Markets
🕐 Apr–Oct Thu 5–10, Sun 4–9

MUSEUM AND ART GALLERY OF THE NORTHERN TERRITORY

This well-planned, modern complex includes the Maritime Museum, a good collection of Aboriginal and Australian art, and displays on local and military history, natural science and Cyclone Tracy (➤ 158). There is a café in the museum.
www.magnt.nt.gov.au
✉ Conacher Street, Bullocky Point ☎ (08) 8999 8201 🕐 Mon–Fri 9–5, Sat–Sun 10–5. Closed Good Fri, 25 Dec 🖐 Free

What to See in the Northern Territory

ALICE SPRINGS

Affectionately known as 'The Alice', this unpretentious Outback town at the heart of the continent was founded as a remote Overland Telegraph station in 1871. Alice Springs is full of attractions: you can take a camel ride, or visit the Old Telegraph Station, the Royal Flying Doctor Service base, a variety of museums and the fascinating Aboriginal Art and Culture Centre.

Nearby, the rugged MacDonnell Ranges contain steep gorges, nature reserves, historic settlements and homesteads, ancient Aboriginal sites, national parks and Palm Valley, where 3,000 rare and ancient palm trees grow.

www.centralaustraliantourism.com

➕ 7B 🚂 The Ghan from Darwin, Adelaide and Sydney ✈ Alice Springs 🛈 Central Australian Tourism Industry Association ✉ 60 Gregory Terrace ☎ 1800 645 199 or (08) 8952 5800 🕐 Mon–Fri 8.30–5.30, Sat–Sun 9–4

DEVIL'S MARBLES CONSERVATION RESERVE

Beside the Stuart Highway to the south of Tennant Creek, these huge, curiously eroded granite boulders are significant in Aboriginal mythology – legend says they are the eggs of the Rainbow Serpent.

www.tennantcreektourism.com.au

➕ 7C 🛈 Tennant Creek Regional Tourist Association ✉ Peko Road ☎ (08) 8962 3388 🕐 Generally Mon–Fri 9–5, Sat 9–12

KAKADU NATIONAL PARK

See pages 46–47.

KATHERINE AND NITMILUK NATIONAL PARK

Katherine, the Territory's third largest settlement, is a pleasant town with a museum, a nature reserve and some historic buildings. The main attraction is nearby Nitmiluk (Katherine Gorge) National Park, with 13 dramatic sandstone gorges. The best way to appreciate Nitmiluk is by taking a cruise on the Katherine River.

www.krta.com.au

🕂 7E 🚆 The Ghan from Darwin and Alice Springs ✈ Katherine
ℹ Katherine Region Tourist Association ✉ Lindsay Street, Katherine
☎ 1800 653 142 or (08) 8972 3249 🕐 Mon–Fri 8.30–5, Sat–Sun 9–2

ULURU–KATA TJUTA NATIONAL PARK

See pages 54–55.

WATARRKA NATIONAL PARK

This remote, rugged desert park, north of Uluru, is famous for Kings Canyon – a spectacular sandstone gorge with walls over 200m (655ft) high. Visitors can explore lush waterholes, wonder at the strangely weathered rocks of the Lost City, and take a challenging bushwalk. There is a wide variety of flora and fauna, including some extraordinary ancient palm trees.

www.nt.gov.au/ipe/pwcnt

🕂 6B 🖐 Free 🚌 None
ℹ Central Australian Tourism Association ✉ 60 Gregory Terrace, Alice Springs ☎ 1800 645 199 or (08) 8952 5800

a drive

Darwin to Litchfield National Park

This drive makes an easy day trip and takes in several attractions outside Darwin, plus a superb national park.

From Darwin's centre, follow the signs to the Stuart Highway and Winnellie.

In the outer suburb of Winnellie, the Australian Aviation Heritage Centre has a good collection of aircraft, including a massive B-52 bomber.

Continue south on the Highway.

Darwin Crocodile Farm, 40km (25 miles) south of Darwin, has over 10,000 saltwater and freshwater crocodiles. This farm and research centre is the ideal place to inspect the most fearsome of reptiles.

Continue south, then take the Berry Springs turn-off.

Berry Springs has two major attractions – the large Territory Wildlife Park, with its excellent collection of native fauna, and the nearby Berry Springs Nature Park, a great spot for a swim or a barbecue.

Return to the Stuart Highway and drive south. Take the Batchelor turn-off.

The small settlement of Batchelor, once a dormitory town for workers at the nearby Rum Jungle uranium field, is best known as the gateway to Litchfield National Park.

Continue for another 21km (13 miles) into the park.

Litchfield National Park, a rugged yet delightful reserve, was little known before the mid-1980s, as it was on private land. Today, visitors come here to enjoy the spectacular waterfalls, refreshing swimming holes, hiking trails and superb views of the region. Other highlights include a small 1930s pioneers' homestead; tall 'magnetic' termite mounds, so called because they always face north–south; and the Lost City, an area of curious sandstone pillars.

Return to Darwin via Batchelor and the Stuart Highway.

Distance 280km (174 miles)
Time A full day is necessary
Start/end point Central Darwin ✚ 6E
Lunch Territory Wildlife Park ($)
✉ Cox Peninsula Road, Berry Springs
☎ (08) 8988 7200

HOTELS

SOUTH AUSTRALIA

ADELAIDE

Hyatt Regency Adelaide ($$$)

Adelaide's finest hotel, right in the heart of the city.

✉ North Terrace ☎ (08) 8231 1234 🚌 City Loop or 99B

Quest Mansions ($–$$)

See page 69.

BAROSSA VALLEY

Novotel Barossa Valley Resort ($$–$$$)

Large resort with fitness facilities and an 18-hole golf course.

✉ Golf Links Road, Rowland Flat ☎ (08) 8524 0000;
www.novotelbarossa.com.au 🚆 Bluebird Barossa Train to Tanunda

NORTHERN TERRITORY

DARWIN

City Gardens Apartments ($$)

Good-value apartments close to the city centre, with a pool.

✉ 93 Woods Street ☎ (08) 8941 2888; www.citygardensapts.com.au

Holiday Inn Esplanade Darwin ($$–$$$)

See page 69.

RESTAURANTS

SOUTH AUSTRALIA

ADELAIDE

North ($–$$)

Modern Australian menu and South Australian wines.

✉ Skycity, North Terrace, Adelaide ☎ (08) 8218 4273;
www.skycityadelaide.com.au 🕐 Lunch and dinner Mon–Sat 🚌 99B, 99C

Botanic Cafe ($$)

Innovative Modern Italian menu, good wine list and great views.

✉ 4 East Terrace ☎ (08) 8232 0626 🕐 Lunch Tue–Fri and Sun, dinner
Tue–Sat 🚌 City Loop

Jolleys Boathouse ($$)

See page 61.

The Oxford Hotel ($$)

A long-running pub restaurant, serving Modern Australian dishes that are deservedly popular with the locals.

✉ 101 O'Connell Street, North Adelaide ☎ (08) 8267 2652 🕐 Lunch Mon–Fri, dinner Mon–Sat 🚌 182, 222

The Oyster Bar ($$)

Relaxed atmosphere. Specializes in a variety of oyster dishes.

✉ 10–14 East Terrace ☎ (08) 8232 5422; www.oysterbar.com.au 🕐 Lunch and dinner Tue–Sun 🚌 99C

BAROSSA VALLEY
1918 Bistro and Grill ($$)

A rustic restaurant serving delicious country-style food.

✉ 94 Murray Street, Tanunda ☎ (08) 8563 0405; www.1918.com.au 🕐 Lunch daily, dinner Mon–Sat 🚌 None

NORTHERN TERRITORY
DARWIN
Cornucopia Museum Café ($$)

Waterfront café in Darwin's premier museum. Good-value meals.

✉ Conacher Street, Bullocky Point ☎ (08) 8981 1002; www.cornucopiadarwin.com.au 🕐 Brunch and lunch daily 🚌 None

The Hanuman ($$–$$$)

Quality Thai and Nonya (Malaysian) cuisine in an elegant setting.

✉ 28 Mitchell Street ☎ (08) 8941 3500; www.hanuman.com.au 🕐 Lunch Mon–Fri, dinner daily

ALICE SPRINGS
Bluegrass Restaurant ($$)

A wide variety of dishes, from kangaroo to vegetarian meals.

✉ Corner of Todd Street and Stott Terrace ☎ (08) 8955 5188; www.bluegrassrestaurant.com.au 🕐 Lunch and dinner Wed–Mon 🚌 None

SHOPPING

ABORIGINAL ART
Framed
Aboriginal art, crafts, sculptures and gifts.
✉ 55 Stuart Highway, Stuart Park, Darwin ☎ (08) 8981 2994 🚌 None

Papunya Tula Artists
See page 73.

OPALS, GEMS AND JEWELLERY
Olympic Opal Gem Mine
✉ 5 Rundle Mall, Adelaide ☎ (08) 8211 7440 🚌 City Loop

Paspaley Pearls
Northern Australian pearls – regarded as the world's finest – and other exquisite jewellery are sold here.
✉ Corner of Bennett Street and The Mall, Darwin ☎ (08) 8982 5555
🚌 None

ENTERTAINMENT

Adelaide Festival Centre
This modern complex is Adelaide's premier performing-arts venue.
✉ King William Road, Adelaide ☎ Box office: 13 12 46 🚌 City Loop

Skycity Adelaide
A casino within the grand 1920s Adelaide railway station.
✉ North Terrace, Adelaide ☎ (08) 8212 2811; www.skycityadelaide.com.au
🕐 Daily from 10am; closed Good Fri, 25 Dec 🚌 City Loop

Darwin Entertainment Centre
A large complex: Darwin's main concert, dance and theatre venue.
✉ 93 Mitchell Street, Darwin ☎ (08) 8980 3333 🚌 None

Skycity Darwin
Beachfront casino complex and popular nightlife venue.
✉ Gilruth Avenue, The Gardens, Darwin ☎ (08) 8943 8888 🕐 Daily

Western Australia

Western Australia takes up almost a third of the continent, but is home to just under 2 million people, the vast majority living in Perth and Fremantle. Much of the terrain is arid and used for little more than cattle farming and mining. The discovery of gold in the southeast in the 1890s initially brought prosperity, and modern Western Australia has boomed because of the extraordinary wealth created by iron ore mining in particular.

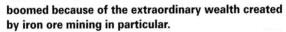

Natural wonders here are remarkable: tall forests in the southwest; a coastline of white sandy beaches and rugged cliffs; extraordinary wildlife, including marsupials like the numbat and quokka, unique to the state; and the dramatic rock formations of the Kimberley in the far north. Many of the southern wild flowers are also found nowhere else in Australia. Although there is much to see, distances are vast – flying is best option for getting around.

www.westernaustralia.com

Perth

Founded in 1829 by free settlers, and initially known as the Swan River Colony, Perth began life as an incredibly isolated outpost of Sydney and the eastern part of the continent. This isolation continues today. Despite its prosperity and cosmopolitan ambience, Perth is the world's most remote city – separated from the east by the desert lands of the Nullarbor Plain, with the nearest large centre, Adelaide, over 2,700km (1,680 miles) away. Much of Perth's charm is due to its location. The city is in a delightful setting on the broad Swan River; some of Australia's best urban beaches lie to the west; and the metropolitan area is backed by the low hills of the Darling Range to the east. The climate is warm and sunny, the generally rather affluent lifestyle is enviable, and the atmosphere is very relaxed for a state capital.

Perth's small and mostly modern city centre, much of which was reconstructed during the 1980s with the proceeds of the state's mineral wealth, offers quite a few attractions of its own. There are historic buildings, many parks and gardens, excellent restaurants and some good nightlife venues. But the true delights of this western capital lie a little beyond the city centre.

Perth is seen at its best from the white sandy beaches of Cottesloe and Scarborough, and on cruises up the Swan River to the vineyards of the fertile Avon Valley. Another highlight is the ferry trip to the atmospheric port town of Fremantle (► 176), 19km (12 miles) downstream.

www.cityofperth.wa.gov.au ✚ 13K

KINGS PARK

Overlooking the city and the Swan River, this popular 400ha (990-acre) reserve consists largely of unspoiled bushland, with colourful wild flowers and prolific birdlife. It also includes the Western Australian Botanic Garden and the State War Memorial. The best way to explore is by renting a bike; or joining a walking tour.

✉ Off Fraser Avenue ☎ (08) 9480 3600 🕐 Daily ✋ Free 🍴 Restaurants ($–$$) 🚌 33 or Perth Tram bus ❓ Free guided walks daily at 10am and 2pm, departing from opposite Visitor Information Centre

ST GEORGE'S TERRACE

A walk along Perth's grandest avenue is the ideal way to see some of the city's historic buildings. Near Pier Street you will find the 1850s Deanery, the neo-Gothic St George's Cathedral, and Government House (1864). Closer to Kings Park are the 1850s Old Perth Boys' School, now owned by the National Trust and also containing a gift shop and café, and the Cloisters, a former collegiate school.

✉ St George's Terrace ◷ Some buildings open weekdays 9–5 ✋ Free 🚌 Central Area Transit bus

WESTERN AUSTRALIAN MUSEUM

Incorporating Perth's original 1850s gaol and an early settler's cottage, this is the state's largest and most comprehensive museum. There are displays on Western Australian mammals, birds and marine life, but the highlight is the Aboriginal gallery. While in this northern city area, visit the Art Gallery of Western Australia, on nearby James Street.

www.museum.wa.gov.au

✉ James Street Mall ☎ (08) 9427 2700 ◷ Daily 9.30–5. Closed Good Fri, 25 Dec, 1 Jan ✋ Donation (moderate for special exhibitions) 🍴 Coffee shop ($) 🚌 Central Area Transit bus

What to See in Western Australia

ALBANY

Now a scenic holiday resort, Albany was Western Australia's first settlement. Founded three years before Perth, the town developed into a port and whaling centre. The old whaling station is now the fascinating Whale World museum, and there is whale watching here from August to October. The town contains the 1850s Residency and Old Gaol, both now museums. The coastline and beaches are spectacular, as is the rugged mountain country of Stirling Range National Park, which lies 100km (62 miles) inland.

www.albanytourist.com.au

➕ 14J ✖ Albany

ℹ Albany Visitor Centre ✉ Old Railway Station, Proudlove Parade
☎ (08) 9841 1088 🕐 Daily 9–5

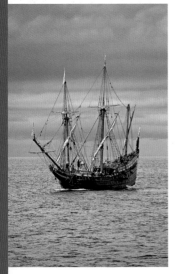

FREMANTLE

Perth's seaport is reached by train or a short boat trip down the Swan River. Fremantle's harbourside location, delightful old buildings and quaint streets make it irresistible. Don't miss the informative Western Australian Maritime Museum, the Fremantle Motor Museum, the markets, the Round House and the austere Fremantle Prison.

www.fremantle.com

➕ 13K 🚉 or ⛴ Fremantle

ℹ Fremantle Tourist Bureau ✉ Town Hall, Kings Square ☎ (08) 9431 7878
🕐 Mon–Fri 9–5, Sat 10–3

KALGOORLIE-BOULDER

Prospectors flocked to this barren Outback region, 600km (372 miles) east of Perth, when rich gold deposits were discovered near Kalgoorlie in 1893. The area still produces nickel and gold. The city of Kalgoorlie and its smaller neighbour, Boulder, contain fine old buildings, the Australian Prospectors and Miners Hall of Fame, at the Hannans North Mine complex, and a Royal Flying Doctor base. The well-preserved ghost town of Coolgardie is also worth a visit.

www.kalgoorlie.com

🚏 15L 🚋 Prospector from Perth ✈ Kalgoorlie

🛈 Kalgoorlie Goldfields Visitor Centre ✉ 250 Hannan Street, Kalgoorlie

☎ (08) 9021 1966 🕐 Mon–Fri 8.30–5, Sat–Sun 9–5. Closed 25 Dec

THE KIMBERLEY

See pages 48–49.

MARGARET RIVER

Some of Australia's best wines are produced around this picturesque town, 280km (174 miles) south of Perth, in over 50 wineries, including the excellent Vasse Felix and Leeuwin Estate. You can sample the wines produced at many of them. The area has wonderful beaches, great surfing and bushwalking along the cliffs of nearby Leeuwin-Naturaliste National Park. The Margaret River township has galleries, craft shops and fine restaurants.

www.margaretriver.com

✚ 13K 🚍 The Australind to Bunbury, then a bus
ℹ️ Margaret River Tourist Bureau ✉ 100 Bussell Highway, Margaret River ☎ (08) 9757 2911
🕐 Daily 9–5

NAMBUNG NATIONAL PARK AND THE PINNACLES

This coastal national park to the north of Perth bristles with thousands of limestone pillars and needles reaching up to 6m (19ft) in height. Early Dutch seafarers believed they had sighted a ruined city, but the Pinnacles are actually the eroded remnants of a former thick bed of limestone. The area has good beaches.

www.calm.wa.gov.au

➕ 13L ✉ Nambung National Park, via Cervantes ☎ (08) 9652 7043

🕐 Daily 🏛 Inexpensive 🚌 None

PEMBERTON

A visit to the small town of Pemberton, at the heart of the southwest's 'Tall Timber Country', reveals a very different aspect of Western Australia. Giant 400-year-old hardwood trees – jarrah, karri and marri – tower 100m (330ft) above the dense undergrowth. Ride the Pemberton Tramway through the forests and visit the local sawmill and a museum.

www.pembertontourist.com.au

➕ 13K 🚌 The Australind to Bunbury, then a bus

ℹ Pemberton Visitor Centre ✉ Brockman Street ☎ (08) 9776 1133

🕐 Daily 9–5. Closed 25 Dec

ROTTNEST ISLAND

This idyllic island lies just 90 minutes by ferry or 15 minutes by air from Perth. First discovered by Dutch seafarers in the 17th century and mistakenly named 'rat's nest' for the quokkas (small marsupials that still roam the island), Rottnest has almost 40km (25 miles) of extraordinarily white beaches, crystal-clear waters that are perfect for fishing, diving and snorkelling, and a relaxed, car-free atmosphere.
www.rottnest.wa.gov.au

✚ 13K 🚢 From Perth, Fremantle or Hillarys Boat Harbour 👆 Ferry fare: expensive (includes entrance fee to island)
ℹ️ Rottnest Island Visitor Centre ✉️ Thomson Bay
☎ (08) 9372 9732 🕐 Daily 8.30–5

SHARK BAY

With islands and 1,500km (930 miles) of indented coastline, the World Heritage Site of Shark Bay, on the state's mid-north coast, is a marine wonderland. This vast inlet is

famous for Monkey Mia beach, where wild dolphins come close to the shore to be hand fed. Visit dazzlingly white Shell Beach and François Peron National Park, and see Hamelin Pool's stromatolites, some of the world's oldest living organisms.
www.sharkbay.asn.au

✚ 1B 👆 Inexpensive
❌ Denham ℹ️ Shark Bay Tourist Bureau ✉️ 71 Knight Terrace, Denham ☎ (08) 9948 1253
🕐 Daily 9–5

WAVE ROCK

This stunning rock formation is one of Western Australia's strangest natural wonders. Wave Rock is a 14m-high (46ft) granite wall, more than 100m (330ft) long, which has been eroded over almost 3,000 million years into the shape of a breaking wave. Other curious (and curiously named) formations in the area include the Breakers and the Hippo's Yawn, and you can also look at Aboriginal hand paintings at Mulkas Cave.

www.waverock.com.au

🚼 14K 🖐 Free 🍴 None

ℹ️ Hyden Tourist Centre ✉️ Wave Rock ☎️ (08) 9880 5182 🕐 Daily 9–5 or 6

a drive south of Perth

Taking in beautiful coastal scenery, this drive can just about be accomplished in a day – or you might want to stay overnight to fully appreciate the area.

Leave Perth via the Stirling Highway, then follow Cockburn Road and Patterson Road to Rockingham.

Make a brief stop at Rockingham, an attractive seaside resort offering excellent beaches and the chance to see fairy penguins at Penguin Island.

Continue south on the Mandurah Road.

Located on the coast at the mouth of idyllic Peel Inlet, Mandurah is the perfect spot for swimming, fishing and boating. There is a wildlife park, a miniature village, and swimming with dolphins in summer.

Continue south on the Old Coast Road.

Yalgorup National Park offers a peaceful environment of swamps, lakes, dunes and woodland. Birdwatchers should look out for some of the 100 or so species of waterbird that frequent the area.

Continue south.

The popular seaside resort of Bunbury has good beaches and a harbour, and you might well see dolphins at Koombana Beach, where the Dolphin Discovery Centre is located. You can drive further south to see the tall 400-year-old trees of the Tuart Forest National Park. If you wish to stay in the area overnight, continue to Busselton and Margaret River (➤ 178).

Head back towards Perth on the fast South Western Highway.

Returning to Perth, stop at the historic town of Armadale (History House Museum), 30km (18 miles) from the city, the Araluen Botanic Park at Roleystone, and Cohunu Koala Park at Gosnells.

Continue on to Perth.

Distance 360km (224 miles) **Time** A full day or more
Start/end point Central Perth ✚ 13K
Lunch Benesse Cafe ($) ✉ 83 Victoria Street, Bunbury
☎ (08) 9791 4030

HOTELS

PERTH
Riverview on Mount Street ($$)
Situated close to the city centre and Kings Park, this hotel consists of self-contained studio apartments.
✉ 42 Mount Street ☎ (08) 9321 8963; www.riverview.com.au 🚌 Central Area Transit bus

KALGOORLIE-BOULDER
Mercure Hotel Plaza Kalgoorlie ($$)
Kalgoorlie's best hotel offers modern comfort and good facilities.
✉ 45 Egan Street ☎ (08) 9021 4544; www.accorhotels.com.au 🚌 None

THE KIMBERLEY
El Questro Wilderness Park ($–$$$)
This vast cattle station provides everything from campsites and bungalows to luxurious rooms.
✉ Gibb River Road, via Kununurra ☎ (08) 9169 1777; www.elquestro.com.au
✖ El Questro Wilderness Park

MARGARET RIVER
Cape Lodge ($$$)
An award-winning lodge with colonial furniture, airy rooms and a rural atmosphere.
✉ Caves Road, Yallingup ☎ (08) 9755 6311; www.capelodge.com.au
🚌 None

RESTAURANTS

PERTH
Dusit Thai ($$)
Perth's Northbridge dining area is full of good restaurants – including this established Thai eatery.
✉ 249 James Street, Northbridge ☎ (08) 9328 7647; www.dusitthai.com.au
🕐 Lunch Tue–Fri, dinner Tue–Sun 🚌 Central Area Transit bus

44 King Street ($$)

Right in the city centre, this brasserie serves a wide range of Mediterranean-inspired snacks and main meals.

✉ 44 King Street ☎ (08) 9321 4476 🕔 Breakfast, lunch and dinner daily 🚌 Central Area Transit bus

Fraser's ($$–$$$)

See page 61.

The Loose Box ($$$)

A half-hour drive from the city, this is arguably Western Australia's best restaurant with classic French cuisine. Award-winning venue with overnight accommodation in luxury cottages.

✉ 6825 Great Eastern Highway, Mundaring ☎ (08) 9295 1787; www.loosebox.com 🕔 Lunch Sun, dinner Wed–Sat 🚌 None

ALBANY

Ristorante Leonardo's ($$)

Serving pastas and Italian steak, vegetarian and seafood dishes, this is one of Albany's most popular restaurants.

✉ 166 Stirling Terrace ☎ (08) 9841 1732 🕔 Dinner Mon–Sat 🚌 None

BUNBURY

Louisa's ($$)

This delightful restaurant in a heritage building offers a Modern Australian menu.

✉ 15 Clifton Street ☎ (08) 9721 9959 🕔 Dinner Mon–Sat 🚌 None

FREMANTLE

Essex Restaurant ($$)

This restaurant, situated in a 100-year-old cottage, specialises in steaks and seafood.

✉ 20 Essex Street ☎ (08) 9335 5725 🕔 Lunch Wed–Fri, Sun; dinner daily 🚌 Fremantle

The Red Herring ($$)

Classy Modern Australian restaurant in a riverside setting, with excellent seafood.

✉ 26 Riverside Road, East Fremantle ☎ (08) 9339 1611; www.redherring.com.au 🕐 Lunch and dinner daily 🚂 Fremantle

KALGOORLIE-BOULDER
Judds Restaurant ($$)

Pub restaurant overlooking Kalgoorlie's main street. Good-value meals. The speciality is wood-fired pizza.

✉ The Kalgoorlie Hotel, 319 Hannan Street ☎ (08) 9021 3046 🕐 Lunch and dinner daily 🚌 None

MARGARET RIVER
Leeuwin Estate Winery Restaurant ($$)

With an emphasis on fresh local produce, this elegant but casual restaurant offers Modern Australian dishes.

✉ Stevens Road ☎ (08) 9759 0000; www.leeuwinestate.com.au 🕐 Lunch daily, dinner Sat 🚌 None

SHOPPING

AUSTRALIANA AND ABORIGINAL ART
London Court

This Tudor-style arcade – a tourist attraction in itself – offers a wide range of souvenir, gift and Australiana-style shops.

✉ Between Hay Street Mall and St George's Terrace, Perth

☎ (08) 9261 6666; www.londoncourt.com.au 🚌 Central Area Transit bus

Creative Native

One of Perth's best Aboriginal art centres, with everything from paintings to silk scarves and jewellery.

✉ 32 King Street, Perth ☎ (08) 9322 3398 🚌 Central Area Transit bus

OPALS, GEMS AND JEWELLERY
Perth Mint
This museum of gold and minting has a shop that sells exclusive jewellery and gifts.

✉ Corner Hay and Hill streets, East Perth ☎ (08) 9421 7223; www.perthmint.com.au 🚌 Central Area Transit bus

DEPARTMENT STORES AND SHOPPING CENTRES
Forrest Chase Shopping Plaza
This large, modern shopping centre is one of the best places to shop in Perth and is conveniently located near the station and northern bus stations.

✉ Murray Street, between Forrest Place and Barrack Street, Perth
☎ (08) 9322 9111 🚌 Central Area Transit bus

ENTERTAINMENT

THEATRE AND CLASSICAL ENTERTAINMENT
His Majesty's Theatre
This charming early 1900s venue is the home of theatre and opera in Perth.

✉ 825 Hay Street, Perth ☎ (08) 9265 0900; www.hismajestystheatre.com.au
🚌 Central Area Transit bus ❓ Friends of the Theatre provide free theatre tours

NIGHTCLUBS AND CASINOS
Margeaux's
A classy nightclub in one of Perth's best hotels; it includes a bar and a disco.

✉ Parmelia Hilton, 14 Mill Street, Perth ☎ (08) 9215 2000 🕐 Daily
🚌 Central Area Transit bus

Index

Acknowledgements

The Automobile Association would like to thank the following photographers, companies and picture libraries for their assistance in the preparation of this book.

Abbreviations for the picture credits are as follows – (t) top; (b) bottom; (c) centre; (l) left; (r) right; (AA) AA World Travel Library; Aust: Australian; SA: South Australia; WA: Western Australia; NT: Northern Territory; Qld: Queensland; Vic: Victoria, NT: Northern Territory; Aust TC: Australian Tourist Commission; WATC: Western Australia Tourist Commission; SATC: South Australia Touist Commission

6/7 Sydney, AA/S Day; **8/9** Finke Gorge National Park, AA/A Baker, **10/11t** Surfers Pradise from Burleigh Heads, AA/A Belcher; **10c** Acacias, AA/A Baker; **10bl** Sydney Harbour, AA/S Day; **10br** Merino sheep, AA/A Baker; **11c** Sydney, AA/S Day; **11b** Sam Lovell, AA/S Watkins; **12** Fish, AA/P Kenward; **12bl** Aboriginal tour, NT, AA/S Watkins; **12/3b** Restaurant, AA/B Bachman; **13t** Menu, AA/L K Stow; **13b** Queen Victoria Market, Melbourne, AA/B Bachman; **14t** Wine, AA/M Langford; **14b** Advert, AA/A Belcher; **15** Café, AA/M Langford; **16t** Sydney Opera House, AA/P Kenward; **16b** Bondi beach, AA/M Langford; **17** Circular Quay, AA/M Langford, **18t** Noosa Heads, Qld, AA/A Belcher; **18c** Koala, AA/A Belcher; **18/9** Ayers Rock, AA/A Baker; **19t** Domaine Chandon Vineyards, AA/B Bachman; **19b** Trekking, AA/M Cawood; **20/1** Milsons Point, AA/ M Langford; **24** National Tennis Centre, Melbourne, AA/ B Bachman; **24/5** Fringe Festival, Melbourne, AA/B Bachman; **26/7** Melaleuca Airstrip, AA/ M Cawood; **28** The Ghan train, AA/ M Langford; **29** Road sign, AA /M Langford; **34/5** Great Barrier Reef, Aust TC; **36** Canyoning, AA/S Richmond; **36/7** Blue Mtns, AA/P Kenward; **38/9t** Kuranda, AA/A Belcher; **38/9b** Port Douglas, AA/A Belcher; **39** (inset) Birdworld, Kuranda, AA/A Belcher; **40** Wet 'n' Wild Water World, AA/A Belcher; **40/1** Warner Brothers Movie World, AA/A Belcher; **41** Currumbin Wildlife Sanctuary, AA/A Belcher; **42** Great Barrier Reef, Aust TC; **42/3** Divers, AA/A Belcher; **43** Townsville, AA/A Belcher; **44/5t** Great Ocean Road, AA/B Bachman; **44/5b** Great Ocean Road, Aust TC/David Simmons; **46** Kakadu National Park, AA/S Watkins; **46/7t** Kakadu National Park, AA/S Watkins; **46/7b** Nourlangie Rock, AA/S Watkins; **48** The Kimberley, Aust TC; **48/9** The Kimberley, AA/S Watkins; **50/1t** Sydney Opera House, AA/S Day; **50/1b** Sydney Harbour, AA/M Langford; **51** (inset) Sydney Opera House, Aust TC; **52/3** Cradle Mountain, AA/S Richmond; **53** Mount Ossa, AA/S Richmond; **54/5** Ayers Rock, AA/S Richmond; **56/7** Great Ocean Road, AA/B Bachman; **58** Bathing, AA/ A Belcher; **59** Dendy Street Beach, Melbourne, AA/B Bachman; **60** Doyle's on the Beach, AA/P Kenward; **62/3** Cape Otway, Aust TC; **64/5** Mount Coot-tha, AA/A Belcher;· **66/7t** Tiwi Islands, AA/S Watkins; **66/7b** AA/B Bachman; **68/9** Hotel, AA/B Bachman; **70/1** Street performer, AA/B Bachman; **72** The Rocks Market, AA/M Langford; **74/5** Sydney Harbour, AA/S Day; **75** Iron railings, AA/S Day; **76/7** The Rocks Market, AA/S Day; **78/9** Walkers near Cradle Mountain, Aust TC; **81** Hunter Valley, AA/S Day; **82/3t** Aust Museum AA/S Day; **82/3b** Darling Harbour, AA/S Day; **84** The Rocks, AA/M Langford; **84/5** The Rocks, AA/M Langford; **85** Sydney Harbour Bridge, AA/P Kenward; **86** Sydney Tower, AA/P Kenward; **87** Taronga Zoo, AA/S Day; **88** National Botanic Gardens, AA/A Baker; **88/9** Aust War Memorial, AA/P Kenward; **90/1** Parliament House, AA/P Kenward; **91** Parliament House, AA/A Baker; **92/3** Byron Bay Lighthouse, Aust TC; **94** Blue Mtns, AA/P Kenward; **96t** Hunter Valley, AA/S Day; **96b** Hunter Valley, AA/S Day; **97** Kangaroo Valley, AA/P Kenward; **98/9** Mt Kosciuszko, AA/S Richmond; **99l** Moss Vale, AA/P Kenward; **99r** Morton National Park, AA/P Kenward; **105** Noosa, AA/A Belcher; **107** Brisbane Botanic Gardens, AA/A Belcher; **108** Mount Coot-tha, AA/A Belcher; **108/9** South Bank, AA/A Belcher; **110/11** Charters Towers, AA/A Belcher; **111** Charters Towers, AA/A Belcher; **112** Fraser Island, AA/A Belcher; **112/3** Fraser Island, AA/A Belcher; **113** Lamington National Park, AA/A Belcher; **114** Noosa, AA/A Belcher; **114/5** Noosa Heads, AA/A Belcher; **115** Pelican, AA/A Belcher; **116/7t** Townsville, AA/A Belcher; **116/7b** Townsville, AA/A Belcher; **117** Whitsunday Islands, AA/ L K Stow; **118** Daintree, AA/A Belcher; **119** Cape Tribulation, AA/A Belcher; **123** St Kilda, AA/B Bachman; **124** Aust Gallery of Sport, AA/B Bachman; **124/5** Melbourne Cricket Ground, AA/B Bachman; **125** Melbourne Museum, AA/B Bachman; **126/7** Melbourne, AA/B Bachman; **127** National Gallery of Vic, AA/A Baker; **128/9** St Kilda, AA/B Bachman; **129t** St Kilda, AA/B Bachman; **129b** St Kilda, AA/B Bachman; **130/1** Yarra River, AA/B Bachman; **131** Royal Botanic Gardens, AA/B Bachman; **132/3** Ballarat, AA/B Bachman; **132** Ballarat, AA/B Bachman; **133t** Dandenong Ranges, AA/B Bachman; **133b** Puffing Billy, AA/ B Bachman; **134/5** Phillip Island, AA/B Bachman; **136** Hobart, AA/A Baker; **136/7** Hobart, AA/A Baker; **138/9** Freycinet National Park, AA/N Rains; **140** Launceston, AA/A Baker; **140/1** Cataract Gorge, AA/A Baker; **142** Port Arthur, AA; **147** Flinders Ranges National Park, AA/M Cawood; **148/9** Atrium of the Art Gallery of SA **149** Front of the Art Gallery of SA **150** Glenelg City in Adelaide in SA, SATC; **152** Adelaide Botanic Garden, North Terrace in Adelaide, SATC/Milton Wordley; **154** National Motor Museum in Birdwood in the Adelaide Hills, SATC/Adelaide Hills Tourism/Adam Bruzzone; **154/5** Adelaide Hills, SATC/Adam Bruzzone; **155** Grant Burge Filsell Vineyard in Barossa, Grant Burge Wines Pty Ltd; **156** Flinders Ranges National Park, AA/M Cawood; **156/7** Flinders Ranges National Park, AA/M Cawood; **157** Kangaroo Island, SA Tourist Board; **158/9t** The Ghan arriving at Darwin Railway Station, Tourism NT/David Silva; **158/9b** Darwin Wharf Precinct, Tourism NT/ Peter Solness; **160/1t** George Brown Darwin Botanic Gardens, Tourism NT; **160/1b** Aerial of Mindil Beach, Tourism NT/Barry Skipsey; **162** Alice Springs, AA/S Richmond; **162/3** Alice Springs, AA/S Richmond; **163** Devil's Marbles, AA/A Baker; **164/5** Kings Canyon, AA/S Richmond; **165** Kings Canyon, AA/ S Richmond; **166/7** Tjaynera Falls, AA/S Watkins; **167** Litchfield National Park, AA/S Watkins; **171** The Kimberley, AA/S Watkins; **172/3t** Swan Bells viewing platform, AA/ M Langford; **172/3b** Perth, AA/ M Langford; **174/5** Kings Park, AA/M Langford; **176** Fremantle, AA/ M Langford; **176/7** Kalgoorlie, AA/A Baker; **178t** Margaret River, AA/M Langford; **178b** Margaret River, AA/M Langford; **179** The Pinnacles, AA/A Baker; **180** Shell Beach, AA/A Baker; **180/1** Wave Rock, WA Tourism; **182/3** Bunbury, WATC.

Every effort has been made to trace the copyright holders, and we apologise in advance for any accidental errors. We would be happy to apply any corrections to following editions of this publication.